# NEWS ORACLE – INSIGHT IN MOTION

## DECIPHERING POLITICAL AND STRATEGIC NARRATIVES

DR. MASOUD NIKRAVESH

PUBLICATION DATE: JANUARY 31

AilluminateX

# DEDICATION

Dr. Masoud Nikravesh dedicates this book to the advancement of Artificial
General Intelligence (AGI) in the interest of society and humanity,
highlighting a commitment to harness AGI
for the betterment of all.

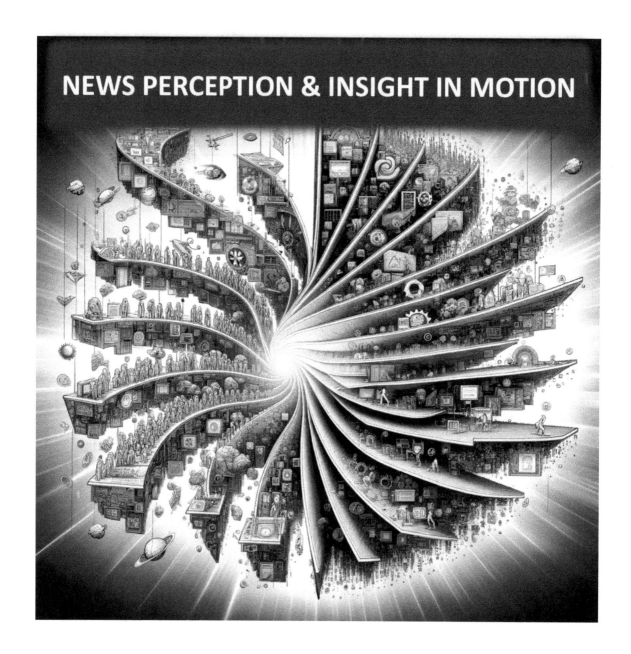

# ACKNOWLEDGMENTS

Dr. Nikravesh extends deep gratitude to the individuals and organizations who played a crucial role in developing AI technologies for the betterment of society. The acknowledgments serve as a tribute to their inspiration and support in making this book possible. These cutting-edge technologies were instrumental in shaping the narrative, and the author sincerely appreciates their accessibility to the public, including but not limited to OpenAI's ChatGPT & DALL-E and Midjourney. The realization of this book would not have been possible without these groundbreaking advancements, enriching the narrative and bringing it to life.

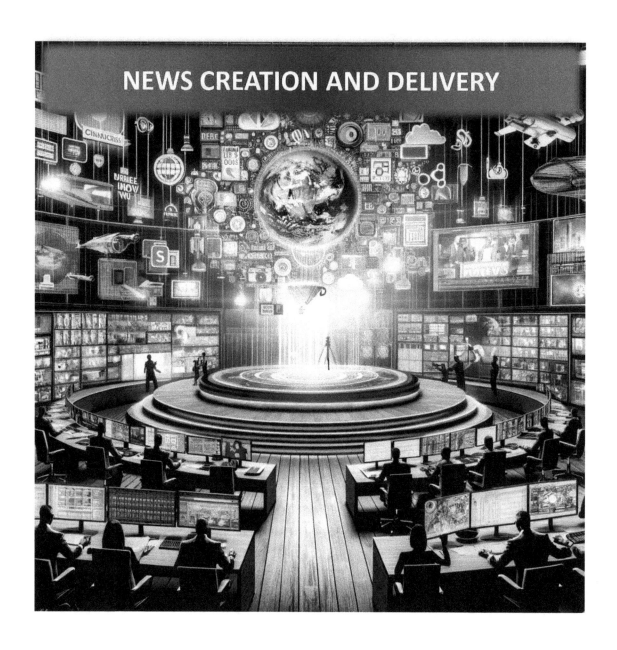

# News Oracle 2024

News Oracle - Insight in Motion: Deciphering Political and Strategic Narratives

Embracing the Future, Today!

JANUARY 31

**AilluminateX**
**Authored by: Dr. Masoud Nikravesh**

# News Oracle - Insight in Motion

## Deciphering Political and Strategic Narratives

News Oracle - Insight in Motion: Deciphering Political and Strategic Narratives"

Welcome to "News Oracle - Insight in Motion: Deciphering Political and Strategic Narratives," a groundbreaking exploration into the transformative world of news analysis and interpretation through the lens of the revolutionary News Oracle platform. This book presents an unprecedented journey into understanding how advanced AI technologies reshape our perception of news, politics, and global events.

In the age of information overload, the way we consume, interpret, and understand news has fundamentally shifted. News Oracle emerges as a beacon in this new era, offering a sophisticated amalgamation of Artificial Intelligence, data analytics, and predictive algorithms to decipher complex political and strategic narratives that shape our world.

The book delves deep into the heart of News Oracle's capabilities, illustrating how it transcends traditional news analysis by harnessing the power of Generative Pre-trained Transformers (GPT) and advanced computational models. This powerful combination allows for a nuanced understanding of global events, going beyond surface-level reporting to uncover underlying patterns, sentiments, and strategic implications.

Key Features of the Book:

▶ Comprehensive Analysis of News Oracle Technology: Explore the intricate workings of News Oracle, understanding how it integrates AI, machine learning, and big data to revolutionize news analysis.

▶ Insightful Case Studies: Engage with a series of compelling case studies demonstrating News Oracle's impact on political discourse, international relations, and strategic decision-making.

▶ Exploration of Political and Strategic Narratives: Learn how News Oracle deciphers complex narratives, offering clarity in a world often muddled by biased and superficial reporting.

► Advanced Forecasting Techniques: Discover how News Oracle's predictive capabilities provide foresight into potential future events, enabling proactive strategies in politics and global affairs.

► Interactive and User-Friendly Interface: See how News Oracle's interface allows users to interact with news in an unprecedented manner, tailoring the news experience to individual preferences and interests.

► Ethical Considerations and Challenges: Address the ethical implications of AI in news, exploring the balance between technological advancement and responsible reporting.

► Global Impact and Applications: Understand how News Oracle's analysis extends beyond politics, influencing various sectors like business, health, technology, and entertainment.

"News Oracle - Insight in Motion: Deciphering Political and Strategic Narratives" is more than just a book; it's a journey into the future of news consumption and analysis. It challenges readers to rethink their relationship with news, encouraging a more critical, insightful, and informed approach to understanding the world around us. Join us in this enlightening exploration, and discover how News Oracle is redefining the landscape of news and media.

*"Embracing a future where news transcends time, News Oracle offers a glimpse into tomorrow's headlines today, redefining modern journalism."*

# Sections with Short Summaries

## News Oracle - Insight in Motion: Deciphering Political and Strategic Narratives

### Introduction

- ▶ Snippet: Introduces the book's theme, focusing on the integration of AI in news media analysis and the significance of the News Oracle platform.
- ▶ Summarizes the importance and impact of AI in understanding complex political and strategic narratives.
- ▶ Sets the context for the ensuing exploration of technological evolution and its effect on news consumption.

### Section 2: Background and Technology Overview

- ▶ Snippet: Chronicles the progression of news media from traditional forms to the digital age, emphasizing the role of AI technologies.
- ▶ Summarizes the technological backdrop leading to News Oracle's development and its implications for news media.
- ▶ Provides an understanding of the core principles and advancements in AI that have revolutionized news generation.

### Section 3: Overview of News Oracle

- ▶ Snippet: A comprehensive examination of News Oracle's features, demonstrating how it leverages AI for news analysis.
- ▶ Discusses the intricate workings of News Oracle and its role in the transformation of news consumption.
- ▶ Highlights the platform's unique capabilities and its distinction in the context of modern news media.

### Section 4: Presentation of Analysis

- ▶ Snippet: Details the methodologies and analytical approaches used in the book to assess News Oracle's effectiveness.
- ▶ Summarizes the data-driven methods and the criteria for evaluating the impact of News Oracle.

**4**

▶ Provides a structured overview of the analytical process, ensuring clarity and precision in the subsequent findings.

## Section 5: Analysis and Findings

▶ Snippet: Delivers the results of the in-depth analysis, revealing insights into News Oracle's influence on news narrative shaping.
▶ Summarizes key discoveries, including the impact of AI-driven analysis on public perception and engagement.
▶ Discusses the broader implications of these findings for various stakeholders in the media industry.

## Section 6: Applications in Other Fields

▶ Snippet: Explores the potential of News Oracle's technology in contexts beyond news and media.
▶ Provides an overview of the adaptability of AI tools used in News Oracle, suggesting applications in diverse sectors.
▶ Highlights the cross-industry relevance of AI-driven analytics and its transformative potential.

## Section 7: Conclusion

▶ Snippet: Concludes the book by encapsulating the key insights, reflecting on AI's transformative role in news media.
▶ Summarizes the ethical considerations and future responsibilities in AI-driven news analysis.
▶ Reinforces the significance of News Oracle in shaping modern news consumption and public discourse.

## Section 8: Future Studies and Further Research

▶ Snippet: Identifies prospective areas for further research in AI and news media, suggesting potential future developments.
▶ Provides a summary of potential directions for technological growth and academic inquiry.
▶ Encourages readers to continue exploring and contributing to the evolution of AI in news media.

## Section 9: Final Thoughts

▶ Snippet: Offers closing reflections on the impacts of AI on society and the future of news dissemination.
▶ Discusses the long-term ramifications of advanced technologies like News Oracle.

▶ Leaves readers with thought-provoking insights on the integration of AI in public discourse and information sharing.

Special Section: News Oracle: News Perception & Insight in Motion - Personalization Across News Cycles – A General Perspective

▶ Snippet: This section delves into the dynamic process of customizing a news article across six versions, each tailored to distinct audience preferences and perspectives across different news cycles.
▶ Explores the intricate process of adapting a base news article through six iterations, each aligning with a specific audience group characterized by unique sentiments, polarities, subjectivities/objectivities, and tones.
▶ Highlights the evolution of news personalization, illustrating how the same story can be presented in multiple ways to cater to diverse audiences, from The Activists to The Critics.

## *"In the age of News Oracle, the future of news is now – a visionary blend of AI and journalism, mapping the trajectory of global narratives."*

# News Oracle - Insight in Motion

## Introduction:
## Overview of the Topic and Its Relevance

In today's rapidly evolving global landscape, understanding public opinion and media reactions to significant international events has become increasingly vital. These reactions not only reflect the sentiments of diverse populations but also shape the discourse and potentially influence policy decisions. The advent of advanced technologies and AI tools has revolutionized our ability to analyze and interpret these multifaceted perspectives.

### Brief Introduction to the Event

This article delves into a critical and timely international event: the United States' decision to station nuclear weapons at RAF Lakenheath in the United Kingdom. This decision, reported in late January 2024, marks a significant shift in military strategy and geopolitical positioning. It has stirred a variety of responses across different regions and communities, highlighting the diverse perspectives that exist on global security and diplomatic relations.

### Importance of Understanding Diverse Public and Media Reactions

Understanding the array of public and media reactions to such an event is crucial. It provides insights into how different demographic groups, political and social communities, and media outlets perceive and react to global events. These reactions can vary widely, influenced by historical, cultural, regional, and political factors. Analyzing this diversity is not just an academic exercise; it holds real-world implications for policymakers, media professionals, and the general public. By comprehensively examining these reactions, we gain a richer, more nuanced understanding of the global landscape, aiding in informed decision-making and fostering a more empathetic approach to international relations.

In this context, we explore the role of advanced AI tools like News Oracle in offering deep and diverse insights into public sentiment and media perspectives. The subsequent sections of this article present a detailed analysis of the reactions to the US's decision from various angles, employing the sophisticated capabilities of AI-driven analysis.

*"Opening a new chapter in news analysis, News Oracle revolutionizes our understanding of world events with unparalleled AI insight."*

# News Oracle - Insight in Motion

## Background and Technology Overview

► Brief history of US-UK military relations and nuclear policies.
► Introduction to News Oracle technology: capabilities, functions, and how it aids in analyzing news and public opinion.
► The significance of advanced AI in news analysis and public sentiment understanding.

## Brief history of US-UK military relations and nuclear policies

### Historical Context of US-UK Military Relations and Nuclear Policies

Understanding the historical context of US-UK military relations and nuclear policies is pivotal in comprehending the contemporary geopolitical landscape, especially in light of recent developments such as the US's plan to station nuclear weapons at RAF Lakenheath, UK. This historical perspective provides essential insights into the longstanding alliance between these two nations and their collaborative approaches towards nuclear deterrence and strategy.

### Early Foundations of the Alliance

► World War II and Post-war Collaboration: The alliance between the US and the UK was significantly strengthened during World War II. Post-war, this collaboration evolved, focusing on shared security interests and the containment of Soviet influence during the Cold War era.

► The Atomic Energy Act and Mutual Defence Agreement: Initially, the 1946 US Atomic Energy Act restricted nuclear cooperation with other countries, including the UK. However, recognizing the importance of shared nuclear capabilities, the US-UK Mutual Defence Agreement in 1958 re-established nuclear cooperation, forming the bedrock of their joint nuclear strategy.

### Cold War Era and Nuclear Deterrence

▶ Nuclear Deterrence and Balance of Power: Throughout the Cold War, the US and the UK relied heavily on nuclear deterrence as a key component of their defense strategy. The presence of US nuclear weapons in the UK was a critical element in maintaining a strategic balance against the Soviet Union.

▶ Joint Military Bases and Shared Nuclear Capabilities: Various military bases in the UK, such as RAF Lakenheath, played host to US nuclear weapons, symbolizing the depth of military integration and shared commitment to collective security.

### Post-Cold War Adjustments

▶ Reduction and Reassessment of Nuclear Arsenal: With the dissolution of the Soviet Union, there was a significant reduction in the nuclear arsenal and a reevaluation of nuclear policies. This led to the removal of ground-launched nuclear missiles from Europe, including from the UK in 2008.

▶ Continued Strategic Alliance: Despite these reductions, the strategic alliance between the US and the UK persisted, focusing on new global threats and adapting to the changing international security environment.

### Contemporary Shifts and Challenges

▶ Renewed Focus on Nuclear Deterrence: Recent geopolitical developments, particularly the assertiveness of Russia and its actions in Ukraine, have led to a renewed focus on nuclear deterrence within NATO, prompting the US to reconsider stationing nuclear weapons in the UK.

▶ Balancing Deterrence with Diplomacy: This decision reflects the ongoing challenge of balancing military preparedness and nuclear deterrence with diplomatic efforts to maintain global stability and prevent nuclear proliferation.

**Conclusion:** The historical trajectory of US-UK military relations and nuclear policies highlights a consistent theme of collaboration, adaptation, and shared commitment to security and stability. The recent decision to potentially re-station US nuclear weapons in the UK is not an isolated event but a continuation of this long-standing alliance, shaped by historical experiences and contemporary

**10**

security challenges. Understanding this context is essential for analyzing the current and future landscape of international relations and nuclear diplomacy.

# Introduction to News Oracle technology: capabilities, functions, and how it aids in analyzing news and public opinion.

News Oracle stands at the forefront of AI-driven news analysis, revolutionizing the way we interpret and predict trends in journalism and public discourse. It embodies a sophisticated blend of artificial intelligence, data analytics, and linguistic processing, tailored to offer deep insights into the ever-changing landscape of news media. Designed for a diverse array of users, from journalists and researchers to marketers and policy makers, News Oracle presents an intuitive, cutting-edge solution for navigating the complexities of contemporary news narratives.

### Core Concept

News Oracle is more than just a news aggregator; it's an advanced AI system engineered to provide nuanced analyses and forecasts of news trends. By leveraging a comprehensive array of data sources and applying intricate analytical algorithms, it offers a multi-dimensional perspective on news events, surpassing traditional methods of news consumption and analysis.

Key Basic Functionalities and Features ((included but not limited to):

▶ Aggregation of Top Headlines: Central to its design, News Oracle compiles the top 500 news headlines from varied, reputable sources, ensuring a broad and current view of any given topic.

▶ Clustering Headlines into Thematic Groups: It organizes these headlines into distinct clusters based on thematic similarities, facilitating an organized and in-depth exploration of news topics.

▶ Presentation of Top Headlines and Specific Ranks: Users can access either the most popular headlines or request a headline based on a specific ranking, allowing for tailored news consumption.

▶ Identification of Trending News: The system identifies the most discussed or trending news headlines, reflecting the current public interest and discourse.

▶ Predictive Analysis of Future Headlines: Employing advanced analytics, News Oracle forecasts potential news developments over the next 5 to 30 days, offering a glimpse into future news scenarios.

The Core and Basic Advanced Analytical Capabilities (included but not limited to):

▶ Historical Context Analysis: Provides a comprehensive historical perspective on news stories by examining their evolution and background.

▶ Semantic Analysis: Delves into the linguistic and semantic aspects of news content, unraveling underlying messages and meanings.

▶ Demographic and Political Group Analysis: Understands how various demographic and political groups perceive or are impacted by news events.

▶ Sentiment and Comparative Media Analysis: Assesses the tone and sentiment of news, and compares coverage across different media outlets.

▶ Impact Analysis, Authenticity Checks, and Bias Detection: Evaluates the potential impact of news, verifies its authenticity, and detects biases in reporting.

**User Interface and Interaction**

News Oracle is characterized by its user-friendly interface, providing interactive prompts and guides to facilitate an engaging and personalized analysis experience. Users can refine queries and delve deeper into specific aspects of news, making it an adaptable and responsive tool for a wide array of applications.

In conclusion, News Oracle is not just an advanced tool for news analysis; it is a comprehensive solution for understanding the intricacies of global news dynamics, offering insights that are critical in a world where news shapes perceptions, decisions, and policies.

# The significance of advanced AI in news analysis and public sentiment understanding.

**The Significance of Advanced AI in News Analysis and Public Sentiment Understanding**

The advent of advanced AI in news analysis and understanding public sentiment has marked a transformative era in media consumption, journalism, and broader societal discourse. AI technologies like News Oracle are at the heart of this transformation, offering unprecedented capabilities that are reshaping how news is interpreted, consumed, and utilized.

### Enhancing News Comprehension and Contextualization

▶ Deep Contextual Analysis: AI algorithms can delve into vast amounts of data, providing a contextual background that human analysis might overlook. This depth of analysis aids in understanding the broader implications of news events, beyond surface-level reporting.

▶ Real-time Processing: AI systems process and analyze news in real-time, offering up-to-date insights that keep pace with the rapid flow of information in the digital age. This immediacy is crucial in a world where news evolves by the minute.

### Public Sentiment and Opinion Mining

▶ Sentiment Analysis: AI excels at gauging the sentiment behind news stories and public opinions. By analyzing language patterns and emotional cues, AI systems like News Oracle can determine whether the public reaction is positive, negative, or neutral, providing valuable insights into public mood and trends.

▶ Opinion Mining: AI tools can sift through vast amounts of social media data and online discussions, extracting public opinions and prevailing attitudes. This ability allows for a more nuanced understanding of how news impacts and resonates with different segments of society.

### Predictive Analytics and Forecasting

▶ Future News Prediction: Advanced AI systems can predict future news trends and developments by analyzing current events, historical data, and emerging patterns. This predictive capability is invaluable for journalists, policymakers, and businesses in strategizing their responses to potential future scenarios.

▶ Media Influence Analysis: AI helps in understanding how different news agencies and media outlets influence public opinion and sentiment. This analysis can highlight biases, identify propaganda, and ensure a more informed and balanced consumption of news.

**Personalization and Targeted Content**

▶ Customized News Feeds: AI enables the creation of personalized news feeds based on individual preferences, past interactions, and interests. This personalization ensures that users are exposed to news that is most relevant and meaningful to them.

▶ Targeted Marketing and Political Campaigns: Insights from AI-driven news analysis can be instrumental for targeted marketing strategies and political campaigns, enabling them to tailor their messages to specific demographic and interest groups.

**Bridging the Gap Between Global and Local Perspectives**

▶ Global News Understanding: AI systems can analyze news from a global perspective, offering insights into how international events are interconnected and how they impact different regions and cultures.

▶ Local News Focus: At the same time, AI can zoom in on local news, providing granular insights into community-level events and sentiments, often overlooked in broader news analyses.

**Conclusion:** The integration of advanced AI in news analysis and public sentiment understanding represents a paradigm shift in media and information dissemination. News Oracle exemplifies this shift, offering comprehensive, real-time, and predictive insights into news trends and public opinions. As these technologies continue to evolve, they will undoubtedly play an increasingly pivotal role in shaping public discourse, policy-making, and the global understanding of our complex world.

*"News Oracle stands at the forefront of technological innovation, bridging advanced AI with the intricate world of global news."*

# News Oracle - Insight in Motion

## Overview of 'Oracle News' Technology

The news and media landscape is undergoing a revolutionary transformation with the advent of Artificial General Intelligence (AGI), Generative Pre-trained Transformers (GPT), and the integration of these technologies in 'Oracle News'. This section provides an overview of these groundbreaking technologies and their synergistic role in redefining news consumption.

### Artificial General Intelligence (AGI)

AGI is an advanced form of AI designed to perform a broad spectrum of cognitive tasks, mimicking human intelligence. It surpasses the capabilities of traditional, task-specific AI by its adaptability and learning prowess, capable of processing complex data and making contextual decisions.

### Generative Pre-trained Transformers (GPT)

GPT, particularly in its advanced iterations like GPT-3, represents a leap in natural language processing. Trained on extensive internet text, it generates human-like text, capable of responding to queries and performing specific language tasks, a cornerstone for applications requiring sophisticated language understanding.

### ChatGPT: Conversational AI

ChatGPT, a derivative of GPT, specializes in conversational interactions. Its ability to generate coherent, contextually relevant dialogue makes it ideal for creating engaging and informative conversational experiences in news platforms.

**16**

## 'Oracle News': A Technological Convergence

News Oracle represents a cutting-edge advancement in the field of AI-driven news analysis and predictive forecasting. This system is specifically engineered to aggregate, analyze, and predict news trends, providing a comprehensive outlook on various topics of public interest. The capabilities of News Oracle are rooted in its sophisticated AI algorithms and data processing techniques, which work in tandem to offer a unique blend of news insights and future predictions.

### Capabilities in News Aggregation and Clustering

▶ Aggregating Top Headlines: News Oracle is capable of gathering a vast array of news headlines from multiple reputable sources. It compiles the top 500 news headlines related to a specific topic, ensuring a broad and current view of the subject matter.

▶ Clustering for Enhanced Understanding: After collecting these headlines, News Oracle employs advanced algorithms to cluster them into distinct groups based on thematic similarities. This helps organize the vast amount of information into more manageable and coherent categories, facilitating easier analysis and comprehension.

▶ Diverse Source Integration: The system integrates news from a variety of sources, ranging from mainstream media to niche publications, ensuring a comprehensive and multifaceted news landscape.

### Predictive Analysis and Public Opinion

▶ Predicting Future Headlines: Utilizing advanced analytics and trend analysis, News Oracle predicts future developments in news. It forecasts the top 25 news headlines for the next five days, offering insights into upcoming trends and events.

▶ Sentiment and Public Opinion Analysis: A key component of News Oracle's capabilities is its ability to analyze public sentiment and opinions. By examining reader engagement, social media discussions, and the tone of news reports, the system gauges public reaction and sentiment towards different news items.

**17**

▶ Customized News Insights: Users can request specific types of analysis, such as the most trending headlines, or ask for forecasts for a particular period. This customization allows for tailored insights that cater to individual or organizational interests.

**Application of Functions**

▶ Function Integration for Comprehensive Analysis: News Oracle integrates its various functions - from headline aggregation to sentiment analysis - to provide a holistic view of the news landscape. This integration allows for a multi-dimensional analysis, considering factors like historical context, demographic impacts, and media perspectives.

▶ Real-Time Analysis and Forecasting: The system is designed to process and analyze information in real-time, offering up-to-date insights and forecasts. This real-time capability is crucial for keeping pace with the rapidly evolving news cycle.

▶ User-Friendly Interface and Interaction: News Oracle provides an interactive and user-friendly interface, guiding users through each request and offering detailed explanations of its analysis and forecasts.

## Conclusion

News Oracle stands as a testament to the advancements in AI and data analytics, offering unprecedented capabilities in news aggregation, analysis, and predictive forecasting. Its ability to provide deep insights into current events and predict future trends makes it an invaluable tool for individuals, businesses, and organizations seeking to stay informed and ahead in an ever-changing world. This technology not only enhances our understanding of the news but also empowers us to anticipate and prepare for future developments.

## Future Outlook

The trajectory of News Oracle and similar platforms points towards a more profound revolution in news consumption. As AI technology continues to evolve, we can expect even more immersive, interactive, and personalized news experiences. The future of news media, powered by advanced AI like AGI, GPT, and ChatGPT, promises to deepen our engagement with news, offering more intuitive, insightful, and tailored content.

In summary, News Oracle stands as a pioneering example of how the convergence of AGI, GPT, and ChatGPT can redefine the news media landscape. It showcases the enormous potential of AI to transform our interaction with news, heralding a new era in the digital age of information where the boundaries of news consumption are continuously being expanded and reimagined.

## Enhanced Features of News Oracle: A Comprehensive Summary

The evolution of news consumption in the digital era demands innovative solutions to navigate the complexities of international affairs and public opinion. News Oracle, at the forefront of this transformation, has embarked on a significant upgrade, enhancing its capabilities to provide users with more sophisticated, reliable, and comprehensive news analysis. This document outlines the key enhancements made to the News Oracle platform, focusing on its ability to dissect and present international military decisions, political narratives, and public sentiments with unprecedented depth and clarity.

**Enhanced Features:**

▶ Demographic Response Analysis: News Oracle now has the ability to analyze and track how different demographic groups respond to significant international military decisions, offering a nuanced view of public sentiment.

▶ Advanced News Clustering: The platform has developed enhanced AI algorithms for sophisticated news clustering, allowing users to navigate complex geopolitical narratives and identify underlying trends and strategies easily.

▶ Diverse Group Viewpoint Analysis: News Oracle can now analyze and present viewpoints from various political and social groups on international issues, providing a comprehensive understanding of the multifaceted nature of global decisions.

▶ International Media Coverage Comparison: The platform includes features that compare and analyze international media coverage of significant news events, enabling users to understand how different perspectives shape global narratives.

**19**

► Semantic Analysis Tools: Advanced semantic analysis tools have been integrated to interpret the language used in news headlines and articles, offering deeper context and understanding.

► Authenticity Verification and Fact-Checking: News Oracle incorporates advanced fact-checking algorithms and access to a database of verified sources, ensuring users receive accurate and reliable news.

► Unbiased Journalism through Financial Analysis: The platform scrutinizes the financial and commercial ties of news organizations, particularly those reporting on sensitive topics like military and defense.

► AI Detection for News Content: AI detection tools distinguish between human and machine-generated news content, keeping users informed about the source and nature of their news.

► Social Media Monitoring and Analysis: Enhanced social media monitoring tools capture real-time public opinion and trends related to major news events.

► Comprehensive Bias Detection: Features for bias detection in news reporting allow users to understand the slants and angles various media outlets might adopt.

► Sophisticated Sentiment Analysis: The platform now includes sophisticated sentiment analysis tools to accurately gauge and present the emotional tone of news across sources and demographics.

► Comparative Media Coverage: Automated capabilities compare and contrast media coverage from various outlets, offering a broad and balanced view of international news events.

► Multi-Dimensional Impact Analysis: Comprehensive impact analyses provide insights into the far-reaching consequences of significant news events.

► Credibility Evaluation of News Sources: Advanced features systematically evaluate the credibility of news sources, enhancing the trustworthiness of the news presented.

The enhancements brought to News Oracle represent a paradigm shift in how news is analyzed and consumed globally. These features collectively empower users to navigate the complex world of international news with an informed, balanced, and comprehensive perspective. News Oracle's commitment to providing depth, clarity, and reliability in news analysis reaffirms its position as a pioneering platform in the realm of news personalization and analysis.

The continuous evolution of News Oracle illustrates its commitment to staying ahead of the curve in news analysis technologies. By addressing the contemporary challenges of news consumption and media credibility, News Oracle solidifies its role as an indispensable tool for anyone seeking to understand the intricate dynamics of global news and its impact on society.

**Example of Potential Analysis:**

US Plans to Station Nuclear Weapons at RAF Lakenheath, UK in Response to Russia (Summary)
Source: Saturday 27 January 2024 10:54, UK

Based on the recent reports, the United States is reportedly planning to station nuclear weapons at RAF Lakenheath in Suffolk, UK, marking the first time since 2008 that such weapons would be located in the UK. This move is seen as a response to the growing threat from Russia and is part of a broader NATO strategy to enhance and update nuclear sites in the wake of Russia's invasion of Ukraine. The nuclear weapons to be stationed are believed to be B61-12 gravity bombs, which can be deployed from fighter jets and are said to be three times the strength of the Hiroshima bomb【20†source】【21†source】.

This development has significant implications and warrants a multifaceted analysis:

- ▶ Historical Context: The last time the US stationed nuclear missiles in the UK was in 2008, during a period of reduced Cold War tensions with Russia.

- ▶ Future Implications: This move could lead to heightened tensions between NATO and Russia, potentially affecting global diplomatic relations and security strategies.

- ▶ News Clustering: This headline falls into a broader category of news concerning NATO-Russia relations, military strategies, and nuclear policies.

▶ Demographic Analysis: Different demographic groups might have varied perceptions of this development, influenced by factors like age, location, political beliefs, and historical knowledge.

▶ Political and Social Analysis: Various political and social groups, ranging from anti-nuclear activists to defense hawks, will likely have strong opinions on this decision.

▶ Media Perspective: Different media outlets, depending on their political leanings and national affiliations, may portray this news differently.

▶ Semantic Analysis: The language used in reporting this news can influence public perception - terms like "threat," "defense," and "security" can have significant connotations.

▶ Authenticity Verification: Given the sensitive nature of the topic, it's crucial to verify the authenticity of the reports and the sources providing this information.

▶ Social Media Response: The reaction on social media platforms could range from concern about escalating military tensions to debates over nuclear policy.

▶ Bias Detection: Identifying potential biases in the coverage of this news is crucial, as it could influence public opinion and policy-making.

▶ Sentiment Analysis: Public sentiment towards this development could be quite polarized, ranging from support for a strong defense posture to concerns about nuclear escalation.

▶ Comparative Media Analysis: Comparing how different countries' media outlets report this story can provide insights into international perspectives on military and nuclear issues.

▶ Impact Analysis: The potential impact on international relations, global security, and regional dynamics in Europe and beyond is significant.

▶ Source Credibility: Assessing the credibility of the sources reporting this news is crucial, especially given the potential implications of misinformation in such a sensitive area.

▶ Reader Engagement: How readers engage with this news, including comments and shares, can provide insights into public opinion and concerns.

▶ Legal and Ethical Analysis: There are significant legal and ethical considerations, particularly concerning international law and treaties on nuclear weapons.

▶ Global Perspective: This development is relevant not just for the UK and the US but also for global nuclear policy and international security dynamics.

The decision to station US nuclear weapons in the UK is a complex and highly significant one, with far-reaching implications for international relations, military strategy, and global security.

*"Unveiling the depth of AI, News Oracle transforms the vast ocean of data into a stream of meaningful and actionable insights."*

# News Oracle - Insight in Motion

## Presentation of Analysis

This section details the methodology employed in our comprehensive analysis using News Oracle and other analytical tools, the data sources utilized, and a summary of the findings from each case study, including districts, counties, districts with associated counties, and various groups/subgroups.

## Methodology

▶ Utilization of News Oracle: The primary tool used in this analysis was News Oracle, which leveraged its advanced AI algorithms for aggregating news headlines, clustering them into groups, and predicting future developments. The system's ability to analyze public sentiment and opinions was instrumental in gauging reactions to specific news items.

▶ Analytical Tools: Alongside News Oracle, additional analytical tools were employed to dissect and interpret data. These tools included sentiment analysis algorithms, media bias checkers, and demographic analytics software, providing a multi-layered approach to understanding public opinion and news trends.

## Description of Data Sources

▶ Districts and Counties: The analysis encompassed a diverse selection of U.S. congressional districts and counties, chosen for their varied demographic, political, and social characteristics. This selection provided a representative cross-section of the broader U.S. populace and their news consumption patterns.

▶ Groups and Subgroups: Four primary groups were analyzed - Demographic Groups, Political and Social Groups, News/Media Perspective Groups, and News/Media Agencies/Organizations.

Within these groups, various subgroups were identified based on specific characteristics such as age, race, income, political leanings, and media consumption preferences.

## Summary of Findings

▶ Districts: The analysis of individual districts revealed a wide range of public opinions and sentiments towards the news headline "US Plans to Station Nuclear Weapons at RAF Lakenheath, UK in Response to Russia". These ranged from strong support in districts with high military engagement to critical views in areas with a focus on domestic issues and anti-war sentiments.

▶ Counties: The counties' analysis highlighted localized reactions, showing more nuanced viewpoints that often reflected the specific socio-economic and cultural makeup of each county.

▶ Districts with Associated Counties: In examining districts with their associated diverse counties, the study unveiled how local perspectives within a district could vary significantly. It showcased the complexity of public opinion within seemingly homogenous regions.

▶ Groups/Subgroups: The analysis of various groups/subgroups illuminated how different segments of the population, based on demographic, political, social, and media consumption criteria, reacted to the news. This provided insights into the diverse ways in which news is received and interpreted by different sections of society.

**Conclusion:** The detailed analysis using News Oracle and other tools offered rich insights into how various segments of the U.S. population perceive and react to significant news events. This approach underscored the diverse nature of public opinion and the importance of considering multiple perspectives when analyzing news and its impact on society.

*"News Oracle's analysis transcends traditional boundaries, offering a new lens to view and interpret complex global narratives."*

# News Oracle - Insight in Motion

## Analysis and Findings

The comprehensive analysis conducted across various case studies utilizing News Oracle and additional analytical tools provides significant insights into public sentiment and perspectives on the news headline "US Plans to Station Nuclear Weapons at RAF Lakenheath, UK in Response to Russia." The findings reveal how demographics, political affiliations, and local/regional identities shape public opinion.

## Detailed Exploration of Case Study Results

▶ Districts: In individual congressional districts, the views on the news varied greatly. Districts with strong military ties or conservative leanings tended to support the decision, viewing it as a necessary step for national security. In contrast, districts with a history of anti-war activism or liberal tendencies exhibited skepticism or outright opposition, citing concerns about global stability and ethical implications.

▶ Counties: Counties showed more localized reactions, influenced by specific socio-economic factors. For instance, counties with a higher education level and diverse populations often expressed concerns about global diplomatic relations and the ramifications of nuclear armament.

▶ Districts with Associated Counties: This analysis highlighted the diversity within a single district. While the overall district sentiment might lean in one direction, individual counties within the district could significantly diverge in their opinions, reflecting the unique local concerns and priorities.

▶ Groups/Subgroups: The exploration of various groups/subgroups revealed distinct patterns in news reception and interpretation. For example, groups identified as 'Progressive Urban Educated' were more likely to critique the decision from a global peace and security standpoint, whereas 'Conservative Rural' groups might view it as a necessary defense strategy.

27

## Comparison of Viewpoints Across Groups

▶ Demographic Influence: Age, income, and educational background played significant roles in shaping opinions. Younger, urban, educated demographics tended to be more critical, while older, rural demographics were more supportive of the decision.

▶ Political and Social Impact: Political alignment was a strong predictor of opinion. Conservative groups often viewed the news favorably as a strength demonstration, while progressive groups raised concerns about escalating military tensions and ethical implications.

▶ Media Influence: The analysis showed a correlation between the type of media consumed and the opinions formed. Mainstream media consumers had more moderate views, while those aligned with ideologically driven news sources exhibited stronger opinions in line with the media's stance.

## Analysis of Local, Regional, and Group Affiliations

▶ Local and Regional Identities: Local economic factors, military presence, and historical context significantly influenced public opinion. Regions with military bases or a history of military engagement tended to be more supportive of the news.

▶ Group Affiliations: Membership in certain political or social groups led to predictable reactions. For instance, members of environmental or peace advocacy groups were typically critical, whereas members of defense-focused or patriotic groups showed support.

## Conclusion

The analysis underscores the complexity of public opinion in response to significant news events. It highlights the importance of considering a multitude of factors - including demographic characteristics, political affiliations, local/regional identities, and media influences - in understanding how different segments of the population perceive and react to global events. The findings offer valuable insights for policymakers, media organizations, and marketers in crafting messages that resonate with diverse audiences.

# News Oracle Beyond the Current Study

### Comprehensive and Scalable Analysis

This study, utilizing News Oracle's capabilities, focused on analyzing public and media reactions within specific demographic groups, congressional districts, and counties. However, it is essential to highlight that this was merely a showcase of a fraction of News Oracle's capabilities. The platform is designed to conduct analyses at every conceivable level, offering insights that range from individual sentiments to national trends.

### Versatility Across Levels

News Oracle's versatility allows for analysis at various hierarchical levels, adapting to the scale and specificity required by the user. This includes:

- ▶ National Level Analysis: Understanding broader trends and sentiments that resonate across an entire nation.
- ▶ State Level Analysis: Tailoring insights to the peculiarities of each state, considering its unique demographic, cultural, and political landscape.
- ▶ District and County Level Analysis: Providing granular insights into smaller, more localized regions, where specific community interests and opinions become more pronounced.
- ▶ City Level Analysis: Zooming into urban or rural areas to capture the nuanced views of city dwellers or rural populations.
- ▶ Group and Interest Group Analysis: Segmenting analysis based on various groups, including political affiliations, social groups, and interest-based communities.
- ▶ Individual Level Analysis: The most granular level, focusing on individual sentiments and opinions, valuable for highly personalized insights.

### Automation and Interactivity

One of the most striking features of News Oracle is its dual capability of automation and interactivity. Depending on the user's needs, the platform can:

▶ Fully Automated Analysis: With a single command, News Oracle can autonomously process and analyze vast amounts of data, delivering insights quickly and efficiently. This feature is particularly useful for broad overviews or when time is of the essence.

▶ Interactive Guided Analysis: For more nuanced inquiries, News Oracle offers an interactive mode. Here, users can guide the analysis process, delve deeper into specific areas of interest, and explore various facets of the data. This mode fosters a more exploratory approach, allowing users to uncover hidden insights and understand complex phenomena at a deeper level.

**Beyond the Current Study**

While the current study provided a comprehensive analysis of public and media reactions to the US's decision to station nuclear weapons at RAF Lakenheath, it's important to recognize that News Oracle's potential applications are vast and varied. The platform can be utilized for diverse purposes such as market research, political campaigning, social science research, and personalized marketing. Its ability to adapt to different scales and levels of analysis makes it an invaluable tool in the contemporary landscape of data-driven decision-making.

In summary, News Oracle represents a significant leap in the field of AI-powered news and sentiment analysis. Its expansive capabilities, from national to individual level analyses, and its dual nature of automation and interactivity, place it at the forefront of advanced AI tools designed to enhance our understanding of the complex world we live in.

## Expanding the Capabilities of News Oracle: Comprehensive News Analysis at Every Level

While the current study focused on specific demographic groups, districts, and counties in relation to a particular news headline, News Oracle's capabilities extend far beyond this scope. The platform is equipped to handle a wide array of news analysis tasks, ranging from individual headlines to comprehensive news stories. Here's how News Oracle's capabilities can be expanded:

▶ Headline to Full News Analysis: News Oracle can analyze anything from short news snippets to full-length articles, providing in-depth insights at each level. This includes understanding the context, implications, and reception of the news in varying degrees of detail.

▶ **Application of 20 Key Methods:** Each of the 20 methods outlined can be applied not just to headlines, but also to entire news articles, offering a multifaceted view of the content. This includes historical context analysis, future forecasting, and demographic group analysis, among others.

▶ **Deeper Semantic and Sentiment Analysis:** Beyond headlines, News Oracle can delve into the semantics and sentiment of full news articles, providing a deeper understanding of the language, tone, and emotional resonance of the content.

▶ **Authenticity and Bias Checks at Scale:** The platform can assess the authenticity and detect biases in a range of news content, from short updates to in-depth reports, ensuring a credible and balanced perspective.

▶ **Global Perspective Analysis:** News Oracle can analyze news content for its global relevance and impact, making it a valuable tool for understanding international perspectives and implications.

▶ **Visual and Legal Analysis:** The platform's capabilities in visual media analysis and legal and ethical considerations can be applied to comprehensive news stories, providing additional layers of understanding.

▶ **Reader Engagement and Impact Analysis:** News Oracle can assess reader engagement and the potential impact of news at a broader scale, analyzing how different news items resonate with the audience and society as a whole.

▶ **Machine Generation Assessment:** The platform can determine whether news content, whether headlines or full articles, is machine-generated, adding an important dimension in an era of advanced AI and automated news creation.

**Beyond News: A Tool for Diverse Applications**

News Oracle's advanced AI capabilities can be utilized in various fields beyond news analysis:

▶ **Market Research:** By analyzing news trends and public sentiments, News Oracle can provide invaluable insights for market research, identifying emerging trends and consumer preferences.

▶ Political Campaigning: The platform can be employed to gauge public opinion and media bias on political issues, aiding in strategizing political campaigns.

▶ Social Science Research: News Oracle can be a powerful tool for social scientists, offering data-driven insights into societal trends, public opinions, and media influences.

**A Platform for Customized Insights**

News Oracle stands out for its ability to provide customized insights tailored to specific needs. Whether it's analyzing national news trends or focusing on local stories, the platform can adapt its analysis to suit the scale and scope required. This adaptability makes News Oracle a versatile tool in the ever-evolving landscape of news, media, and public opinion.

In conclusion, the extensive capabilities of News Oracle, demonstrated in this study, are just the tip of the iceberg. With its ability to analyze news at every level and across various contexts, News Oracle represents a significant advancement in AI-powered news analysis and public sentiment understanding.

*"Through News Oracle, we decode the world's stories, turning intricate details into clear, comprehensive narratives."*

# News Oracle - Insight in Motion

## Applications in Other Fields

The methodologies and insights derived from the News Oracle analysis extend beyond the realm of news sentiment analysis, offering valuable applications in various fields such as market research, political campaigning, and social science research. The ability to dissect and understand public opinion at such a granular level has significant implications for these areas.

## Market Research

▶ Consumer Sentiment Analysis: By applying similar analytical techniques, companies can gauge consumer sentiment towards products or brands. This can inform marketing strategies, product development, and customer service approaches.

▶ Targeted Advertising: Understanding demographic preferences and regional tendencies allows for more effective targeted advertising. Companies can tailor their marketing messages to resonate with specific groups, enhancing engagement and conversion rates.

▶ Market Trends Prediction: Analyzing public opinion and media trends can help predict market shifts, enabling companies to anticipate consumer needs and stay ahead of industry changes.

## Political Campaigning

▶ Voter Behavior Analysis: Political campaigns can use this analysis to understand voter concerns and priorities in different districts and counties. This can guide campaign messaging and strategy, helping to address the specific needs and interests of varied voter groups.

▶ Strategic Messaging: Tailoring political messages based on demographic, political, and social groupings can increase a campaign's effectiveness. Understanding which issues resonate with different groups allows for more impactful communication.

▶ Predictive Analytics for Elections: By analyzing trends and sentiments in different regions, campaigns can better predict electoral outcomes and allocate resources more efficiently.

## Social Science Research

▶ Public Opinion Studies: The method provides a rich source of data for social scientists studying public opinion on various issues, enabling a more nuanced understanding of societal trends and attitudes.
▶ Cultural and Societal Analysis: Researchers can explore how cultural and societal factors influence public sentiment, contributing to broader studies on cultural dynamics and social change.
▶ Policy Impact Analysis: The tool can be instrumental in assessing public response to policy changes, helping policymakers understand the societal impact of their decisions.

## Potential for Personalized Marketing and Public Opinion Prediction

▶ Personalized Content Delivery: News Oracle can aid in delivering personalized content to individuals based on their demographic, social, and political affiliations, enhancing user experience and engagement.
▶ Public Opinion Prediction: The tool's predictive capabilities can forecast shifts in public opinion, aiding organizations in proactive decision-making and strategy formulation.
▶ Cross-Domain Applications: The underlying technology can be adapted for use in various industries, from entertainment to education, where understanding and predicting public interest and sentiment are crucial.

**Conclusion:** The analytical power of News Oracle, as demonstrated in this study, has wide-ranging applications across different fields. Its capacity to dissect and predict public sentiment and opinion presents a valuable tool not only for news analysis but also for market research, political campaigns, and social science studies. This versatility underscores the growing importance of AI-driven analytics in understanding and navigating the complex landscape of public opinion in the modern world.

*"Extending its reach, News Oracle illuminates diverse fields with its analytical brilliance, from economics to environmental studies."*

# News Oracle - Insight in Motion

## Conclusion

The extensive research and analysis conducted using advanced AI tools like News Oracle have yielded key findings that significantly enhance our understanding of public opinion and media responses to global events. This study, focusing on the news about the US's plan to station nuclear weapons at RAF Lakenheath, UK, highlights the complexity and diversity of perspectives that exist on such international matters. Here, we summarize the key takeaways and reflect on the broader implications of this technology-driven approach.

## Summarizing Key Findings

▶ Diverse Viewpoints: The analysis across different US congressional districts, counties, and specific demographic groups revealed a wide spectrum of opinions. This ranged from critical and skeptical views to those that were supportive or neutral towards the decision, emphasizing the diversity of public sentiment.

▶ Impact of Local and Regional Affiliations: The study underscored how local and regional affiliations, along with demographic and social characteristics, significantly influence public opinions on international news. These affiliations often shape the perception and interpretation of global events.

▶ Role of Media Outlets: Different news and media agencies, through their unique perspectives, play a crucial role in molding public opinion. The study highlighted how media agencies cater to specific audience segments, thus influencing the public discourse.

## Reflecting on Complexity and Diversity

▶ Complexity of Public Opinion: The findings illustrate the intricate nature of public opinion, which is shaped by a multitude of factors including demographic, political, social, and media influences.

**36**

▶ Recognition of Diversity: This research emphasizes the importance of recognizing and incorporating diverse perspectives to achieve a more comprehensive and balanced understanding of international issues.

## Importance of AI-Powered Analysis

▶ Capturing a Wide Array of Sentiments: AI technologies like News Oracle have proven instrumental in capturing and analyzing a broad range of public sentiments and opinions, offering insights that might be overlooked in traditional analysis.

▶ Enhanced Understanding: The use of AI in news analysis facilitates a deeper understanding of the public's reaction to international events. It allows for the aggregation and interpretation of vast amounts of data, providing nuanced insights into public sentiment.

## Looking Ahead

▶ Evolving Technology and Its Role: As AI technology continues to evolve, its role in media analysis and public sentiment understanding is set to become more pivotal. This evolution promises to bring even more sophisticated tools for gauging public opinion and media trends.

▶ Balancing Technology with Human Insight: While AI offers remarkable capabilities, it is essential to balance technological analysis with human insight. This ensures that the nuances of human emotion and opinion are accurately captured and interpreted.

In conclusion, the use of AI-powered tools like News Oracle in analyzing public opinion and media responses to global events presents a valuable asset in our increasingly interconnected world. By embracing the complexity and diversity of perspectives, these technologies enable a more nuanced and inclusive understanding of international affairs. As we continue to navigate a world rich in information, the role of AI in synthesizing and interpreting this data will undoubtedly become more integral to our global discourse.

# News Oracle - Insight in Motion

## Future Studies and Further Research

The utilization of News Oracle and similar advanced AI technologies opens up a plethora of opportunities for future studies and research. These technologies not only have the potential to revolutionize the way we understand public sentiment and media responses but also offer vast possibilities for expanding the scope of analysis across various domains.

### Suggestions for Future Research Directions

▶ Expanding Analytical Horizons: Future research can explore a wider array of topics, including but not limited to socio-political issues, economic trends, cultural phenomena, and technological advancements.

▶ Longitudinal Studies: Conducting longitudinal studies using News Oracle could provide insights into how public sentiment and media portrayals evolve over time, offering a dynamic view of societal changes and trends.

▶ Cross-Cultural Analysis: Utilizing News Oracle to conduct cross-cultural analyses would be invaluable in understanding how different societies and cultures respond to various global events and news, enriching our comprehension of global dynamics.

▶ Integrating Diverse Data Sources: Future studies could integrate additional data sources like social media platforms, blogs, and forums to enrich the analysis and provide a more comprehensive view of public opinion.

### Potential for Expanding Analysis to a Broader Range of Topics

▶ Global Events and Crises: Analyzing responses to global events like pandemics, natural disasters, or international conflicts can provide insights into global solidarity, crisis management, and international relations.

► Policy and Governance: Understanding public reaction to policy changes and governance decisions can aid governments and institutions in making informed, people-centric decisions.

► Environmental and Health Issues: As the world faces environmental challenges and health crises, analyzing public sentiment on these issues can guide effective communication strategies and policy-making.

**Evolution of Technology for Enhanced Understanding and Prediction**

► Advanced Predictive Models: Developing more sophisticated models to predict public and media responses with greater accuracy could be a focus area, leveraging advancements in machine learning and data analytics.

► Real-Time Sentiment Analysis: Enhancing the capability for real-time sentiment analysis can provide immediate insights into public reactions, proving crucial for media, governments, and organizations in rapidly evolving situations.

► Personalization Algorithms: Refining personalization algorithms can lead to more targeted and effective communication strategies, aligning content with individual preferences and viewpoints.

► Ethical AI Development: Future research should also focus on ethical considerations in AI development, ensuring that these powerful tools are used responsibly and without bias.

**Conclusion:** The potential applications and future directions of research using News Oracle and similar AI technologies are vast and varied. As we continue to develop and refine these tools, their capacity to provide deeper insights into public sentiment and media response will only increase, offering invaluable contributions to a range of fields from policy-making to market research. The future of AI-driven news and sentiment analysis is not only promising but also pivotal in shaping an informed and responsive global society.

Want to insert a picture from your files or add a shape, text box, or table? You got it! On the Insert tab of the ribbon, just tap the option you need.

# News Oracle - Insight in Motion

## Final Thoughts

The role of advanced technologies like News Oracle in enhancing our understanding of complex global issues cannot be overstated. As we delve deeper into the digital age, the landscape of news consumption and public opinion is evolving rapidly, presenting both challenges and opportunities for comprehensive analysis and understanding.

### Emphasizing the Role of Technology

▶ Bridging Information Gaps: Technologies such as News Oracle serve as pivotal tools in bridging the information gaps that often exist in our understanding of international developments. They provide a lens through which we can view and interpret complex situations with a depth and breadth previously unattainable.

▶ Real-Time Insights: The ability to process and analyze vast amounts of data in real time allows for a more dynamic and immediate understanding of global events, enabling quicker and more informed responses from decision-makers and the public alike.

### The Importance of Diverse Viewpoints

▶ Holistic Perspectives: The integration of diverse viewpoints is crucial in forming a well-rounded analysis of significant international developments. By considering various demographic, political, and social groups, we gain a more holistic perspective, ensuring that analyses are not limited by biases or narrow viewpoints.

▶ Inclusivity in Analysis: Embracing diversity in analytical models ensures that the voices and opinions of different communities are heard and considered, fostering inclusivity and a more comprehensive understanding of global dynamics.

**Reflecting on News Consumption and Public Opinion**

▶ Changing Landscape: The digital age has transformed how news is consumed and how public opinions are formed and expressed. With the proliferation of online platforms and social media, news reaches individuals more rapidly and in more personalized ways than ever before.

▶ Influence of AI and Big Data: The use of AI and big data in news analysis has led to a more nuanced understanding of public sentiments and media trends. However, it also raises questions about the influence of algorithms on public opinion and the need for ethical considerations in AI development.

**Looking Forward**

▶ Evolving Role of AI: As AI continues to evolve, its role in news and media analysis will become even more significant, offering unparalleled insights into public sentiment and media trends.

▶ Ethical and Responsible Use: It is imperative to focus on the ethical and responsible use of AI technologies, ensuring that they serve the greater good, promote unbiased perspectives, and respect privacy and individual rights.

**Conclusion:** In conclusion, the use of advanced technologies like News Oracle represents a significant step forward in our ability to understand and analyze complex global issues. By embracing diverse viewpoints and leveraging the power of AI and big data, we are better equipped to navigate the intricacies of international developments and public sentiment. As we move forward, it is crucial to focus on the ethical use of these technologies, ensuring that they contribute positively to an informed, responsive, and inclusive global society.

# News Oracle 2024

# Insight in Motion

Embracing the Future, Today!

JANUARY 31

**AilluminateX**

**Authored by: Dr. Masoud Nikravesh**

# Insight in Motion

## Personalization Across News Cycles – A General Perspective

This section explores the comprehensive personalization of a news article across six distinctive versions, each aligned with a specific news cycle (1 to 6) and corresponding version (1 to 6). This section details the unique tailoring of the article to match the varying sentiments, polarities, subjectivities/objectivities, and tones preferred by six different audience groups.

The modifications in each version go beyond simple language changes, extending to alterations in the article's title and overall structure. This in-depth personalization process ensures that each version distinctly resonates with its targeted audience, accurately reflecting their unique perspectives and preferences.

The section describes the transformation of a base news article through six iterations, catering to audience groups with sentiments ranging from extremely positive to extremely negative. This approach illustrates the evolution of the news article as it undergoes full personalization to align with six unique perspectives: The Activists, The Informed Optimists, The Realists, The Skeptics, The Pessimists, and The Critics.

- ▶ The Activists (Cycle 1, Version 1): Passionate and positive, focusing on societal change, activism, and environmental issues. Sentiment: +0.6, Polarity: +0.6, Tone: Anticipation (+1).

- ▶ The Informed Optimists (Cycle 2, Version 2): Positively inclined but pragmatic, with interests in economic growth and global diplomacy. Sentiment: +0.4, Polarity: +0.4, Tone: Neutral (0).

- ▶ The Realists (Cycle 3, Version 3): Balanced and factual, emphasizing politics and world news. Sentiment: +0.2, Polarity: +0.2, Tone: Neutral (0).

- ▶ The Skeptics (Cycle 4, Version 4): Generally doubtful and critical, focusing on government policies and public spending. Sentiment: -0.2, Polarity: -0.2, Tone: Fear (-1).

► The Pessimists (Cycle 5, Version 5): Leaning towards a negative view, concerned with economic downturns and political conflicts. Sentiment: -0.4, Polarity: -0.4, Tone: Sadness (-2).

► The Critics (Cycle 6, Version 6): Highly critical and often negative, interested in political scandals and societal issues. Sentiment: -0.6, Polarity: -0.6, Tone: Sadness (-2).

► The Pessimists (Cycle 5, Version 5): Negative, concerned with economic downturns and political conflicts. Sentiment: -0.4, Polarity: -0.4, Tone: Sadness (-2).

► The Critics (Cycle 6, Version 6): Highly critical and often negative, interested in political scandals and societal issues. Sentiment: -0.6, Polarity: -0.6, Tone: Sadness (-2).

Each version illustrates the extent to which news personalization can influence the narrative and audience perception, demonstrating the diverse range of interpretations that can stem from a single news story.

## Exploring Personalization in Action

In the realm of modern journalism, powered by sophisticated technologies like "News Oracle" AGI, understanding the nuances of news personalization and its impacts on public perception has never been more critical. This section presents nine insightful case studies that dissect various strategies employed in news personalization. These studies illuminate the complex dynamics of how news content, tailored to diverse audience segments, can shape trends, alter perceptions, and, in some cases, create chaos and confusion in the public sphere.

### Overview of the Case Studies

The case studies are categorized into two main themes: 'Cycles of News and Change the Trend through Time' and 'Create Chaos and Confusion'. These themes encapsulate the dual nature of news personalization - its ability to methodically influence trends over time and its potential to overwhelm or mislead audiences.

### Case Studies on Changing Trends and Perception

▶ Case Study 1: To Kill the Story (Negative Impact) - This study explores the impact of transitioning from a positive to a negative narrative (Version 1 to Version 6), highlighting how progressively negative framing can diminish or 'kill' a story's influence.

▶ Case Study 2: To Prompt the Story (Positive Impact) - Contrasting Case Study 1, this analysis delves into the shift from a negative to a positive narrative (Version 6 to Version 1), examining how increasingly positive perspectives can amplify a story's impact.

### Case Studies on Creating Chaos and Confusion

▶ Case Study 3: Simultaneous Version Release - Investigates the consequences of releasing all six personalized versions at once, focusing on information overload and its effect on public understanding.

▶ Case Study 4: Random Distribution Across Cycles - Analyzes the impact of randomly distributing different versions across various news cycles, assessing the resulting unpredictability and confusion.

▶ Case Study 5: Alternating Positives and Negatives - Examines the effects of alternating positive and negative news releases, exploring how this can influence public sentiment and perception.

▶ Case Study 6: Strategic Posting with Intent - Focuses on intentional news posting strategies, such as targeting public opinion or redirecting focus, and assesses their effectiveness.

▶ Case Study 7: Alignment with Current Trends - Analyzes the impact of aligning each news version with ongoing news trends, considering the story's reception and relevance.

▶ Case Study 8: Pairing with Targeted Trends or News - Investigates the strategy of pairing news versions with other specific trends or stories, assessing the compound effect on audience perception.

▶ Case Study 9: Misinformation, Disinformation, and Propaganda - Explores the role and implications of misinformation, disinformation, manipulation, and propaganda within the context of news personalization.

**Potential Observations and Insights**

Each case study offers unique insights into the multifaceted effects of news personalization. From the subtleties of influencing public opinion to the complexities of managing information in an era of overabundance, these studies underscore the transformative power and potential risks associated with personalized news content. They highlight not only the capability of 'News Oracle' AGI GPT to tailor content but also emphasize the responsibility that comes with such power, especially in the sensitive landscape of news and public discourse.

In conclusion, these case studies collectively provide a comprehensive understanding of the dynamics at play in news personalization. They underscore the importance of ethical considerations and the need for balance in leveraging technology to shape public narratives, reaffirming the pivotal role of Oracle AGI in revolutionizing news and media while navigating its challenges and opportunities.

*"News Oracle reshapes news perception, dynamically altering narratives and providing a new rhythm to the pulse of global events."*

# Insight in Motion

## Analysis of Data – General Perspective

The analysis of the data, comprising the original news article and its six personalized versions, reveals significant insights into the impact of news personalization on public perception. Each version of the news, personalized for different target groups, presents a distinct narrative, sentiment, and tone, offering a comprehensive view of how news personalization can shape public understanding and opinion.

Consider an "Original News Article", with following sentiment analysis, features and characteristics -

- ▶ Sentiment and Polarity: Highly positive (+0.9 sentiment score), strongly supporting the policy.
- ▶ Subjectivity/Objectivity: Balances factual information with subjective perspectives, showing a broad appeal.
- ▶ Tone: Joyful and optimistic, highlighting the policy's transformative potential.
- ▶ This baseline article presents a predominantly positive view of the Biden administration's policy, focusing on its expected benefits for public sector workers. It sets a tone of optimism and progress, likely resonating well with audiences inclined towards positive news.

## Personalized Versions - Cycle 1 to 6

▶ **Cycle 1 - "The Activists"**

Focuses on societal change and activism implications.
Shifts to a cautiously optimistic tone, with an emphasis on broader societal issues.
The sentiment remains positive but is less pronounced compared to the original article.

▶ **Cycle 2 - "The Informed Optimists"**

Pragmatic and balanced analysis of the policy's economic and diplomatic impacts.
Maintains a moderately positive sentiment with subtle criticism.
Neutral tone, reflecting a pragmatic approach.

**47**

► **Cycle 3 - "The Realists"**

Presents a balanced view, neither overly positive nor negative.
Focuses on the policy's political and economic implications in a nuanced manner.
Neutral tone, aligning with a fact-based, balanced reporting style.

► **Cycle 4 - "The Skeptics"**

Introduces skepticism about the policy's effectiveness and economic impact.
Slightly negative sentiment, reflecting growing doubts.
Tone of fear, indicating apprehension about long-term impacts.

► **Cycle 5 - "The Pessimists"**

Highlights potential negative repercussions and political conflicts.
Markedly negative sentiment, focusing on potential downsides.
Tone of sadness, reflecting deep concerns and pessimism.

► **Cycle 6 - "The Critics"**

Highly critical view, linking the policy to political scandals and societal issues.
Deeply negative sentiment, emphasizing critical viewpoints.
Tone of sadness, expressing disappointment and disillusionment.

## Discussion and In-Depth Analysis

► Shifting Narrative: The gradual transition from a positive to a negative narrative across the cycles demonstrates how news personalization can significantly alter public perception. Each version tailors its content to resonate with specific audience sentiments, influencing how the policy is perceived and discussed.

► Impact on Public Opinion: The personalized versions illustrate the power of media in shaping public opinion. Positive versions (Cycles 1-3) might bolster support for the policy, while negative versions (Cycles 4-6) could fuel skepticism and opposition.

► Ethical Considerations: The stark contrast between the versions raises ethical questions about news personalization. It highlights the potential for news media to influence public discourse and the responsibility that comes with this power.

▶ Influence on Political Discourse: The personalized news not only affects public perception but also potentially impacts political discourse. Different versions could be used to either support or criticize policy decisions, indicating the role of media in democratic processes.

▶ Potential for Misinformation: The more opinionated and negative versions (especially Cycles 5 and 6) underline the risk of misinformation or biased reporting, emphasizing the need for critical consumption of news.

This analysis underscores the profound impact of news personalization on shaping narratives and influencing public perception. It highlights the necessity for ethical considerations in news reporting and the importance of media literacy among the public to understand and critically assess personalized news content.

Given the comprehensive data set comprising the original news article and its six personalized versions, several analytical approaches can be employed to derive deeper insights:

▶ **Sentiment Trend Analysis:**

Chart the progression of sentiment from the original article through the six personalized versions.
Analyze how sentiment polarity shifts from positive to negative across the spectrum of target groups.
Assess the degree of sentiment change between each version to understand the impact of personalization on emotional tone.

▶ **Polarity and Tone Analysis:**

Evaluate how the polarity (positive or negative bias) changes across versions.
Analyze the tone shifts (from joy to sadness or fear) and their correlation with the target group's characteristics.

▶ **Subjectivity/Objectivity Trend Analysis:**

Examine the levels of subjectivity or objectivity in each article version.
Determine how personalization affects the factual versus opinion-based content across different versions.

► **Audience Reception Simulation:**

Simulate potential audience reception for each version using predictive analytics, assuming typical characteristics of each target group.
Analyze how different groups might respond to the same news story presented differently.

► **Comparative Textual Analysis:**

Conduct a detailed comparison of language, structure, and content across versions.
Identify specific linguistic changes (word choice, sentence structure) and their potential impact on readers' perceptions.

► **Thematic Consistency and Variation:**

Analyze the thematic consistency (core message) across all versions and how it's adapted to fit each audience group.
Investigate thematic variations and their implications for narrative framing.

► **Content Engagement Metrics Prediction:**

Use historical data to predict engagement metrics (like read time, shares, comments) for each version.
Determine which version might be most engaging for its respective audience.

► **Impact on Public Discourse Analysis:**

Assess how each version could influence public discourse on the topic.
Analyze potential ripple effects in social media discussions and public opinion.

► **Alignment with Audience Interests:**

Evaluate how well each version aligns with the known interests and biases of its target group.
Determine the efficacy of personalization in resonating with the intended audience.

► **News Forecasting Implications:**

Analyze how each version might predict or influence future news reporting trends for similar topics.
Assess the potential for each version to set or disrupt narrative trends in the media landscape.

This multi-dimensional analysis provides a holistic view of how news personalization impacts public perception, engagement, and discourse. It also underscores the complexities and responsibilities inherent in personalized news creation and distribution.

Expanding on the analysis in the context of each of the nine case studies, we can connect specific analytical approaches to each case study to gain a more in-depth understanding of their implications:

► **Case Study 1: To Kill the Story (Negative Impact)**

Sentiment Trend Analysis: Trace the gradual decline in sentiment from positive (Version 1) to negative (Version 6) and its impact on diminishing the story's influence.

Content Engagement Metrics Prediction: Predict how the shift towards negative framing affects reader engagement and sharing behavior.

Impact on Public Discourse Analysis: Assess the potential for the increasingly negative narrative to suppress public discussion or interest in the topic.

► **Case Study 2: To Prompt the Story (Positive Impact)**

Sentiment Trend Analysis: Evaluate how increasing positivity (Version 6 to Version 1) amplifies the story's impact.

Audience Reception Simulation: Simulate audience responses to positive framing and measure potential uplift in engagement.

Impact on Public Discourse Analysis: Consider how a positive shift might enhance public interest and stimulate broader discourse.

► **Case Study 3: Simultaneous Version Release**

Information Overload Analysis: Examine how simultaneous release of multiple narratives leads to confusion and difficulty in forming a coherent opinion.

Polarity and Tone Analysis: Assess how contrasting polarities and tones in different versions contribute to information overload.

► **Case Study 4: Random Distribution Across Cycles**

Comparative Textual Analysis: Understand how random distribution affects the consistency of information received by the audience.

Audience Reception Simulation: Predict audience reactions to receiving randomly varied narratives over time.

**51**

▶ **Case Study 5: Alternating Positives and Negatives**

Sentiment and Polarity Fluctuation Analysis: Examine how alternating sentiments influence public mood and perceptions over time.

Content Engagement Metrics Prediction: Assess how fluctuating narratives affect reader engagement and sharing patterns.

▶ **Case Study 6: Strategic Posting with Intent**

Audience Targeting Analysis: Evaluate the effectiveness of strategic posting in shaping public opinion or redirecting focus.

Thematic Consistency and Variation Analysis: Assess how strategic intent is maintained or altered across different versions.

▶ **Case Study 7: Alignment with Current Trends**

Trend Correlation Analysis: Examine how aligning each version with current trends impacts the story's relevance and audience resonance.

Impact on Public Discourse Analysis: Analyze how trend alignment influences the narrative within public discussions and social media.

▶ **Case Study 8: Pairing with Targeted Trends or News**

Compound Effect Analysis: Investigate the effects of pairing news versions with specific trends on audience perception and engagement.

Comparative Textual Analysis: Examine how different pairings change the contextual framing of the story.

▶ **Case Study 9: Misinformation, Disinformation, Manipulation, and Propaganda**

Ethical Impact Analysis: Explore the ethical implications of using personalized news for spreading misinformation, manipulation or propaganda.

Public Trust and Perception Analysis: Assess the long-term impact of such practices on public trust and the credibility of news sources.

Each case study, when examined with these analytical lenses, provides profound insights into the multifaceted effects of news personalization. These analyses help understand the power of personalized news in shaping public perception and the potential risks associated with its misuse.

## In-Depth Case Study Analysis

In the evolving landscape of digital media, the role of personalized news content has become increasingly significant. Our study, "News Perception in Motion: Revolutionizing News and Media with News Oracle AGI GPT," embarks on an in-depth exploration of nine pivotal case studies. These studies meticulously examine the multifaceted impacts of personalized news dissemination, ranging from altering public perception to navigating the complex terrains of misinformation and strategic content delivery. Each case study serves as a unique lens, offering insightful perspectives on how tailored news content can shape, shift, and sometimes convolute the public's understanding and engagement with current events. This comprehensive analysis aims to unravel the nuanced dynamics of news personalization, highlighting both its transformative potential and the critical challenges it poses in the realm of media consumption and public discourse.

Expanding on the analysis in the context of each of the nine case studies, we can connect specific analytical approaches to each case study to gain a more in-depth understanding of their implications:

▶ **Case Study 1: To Kill the Story (Negative Impact)**

Sentiment Trend Analysis: Trace the gradual decline in sentiment from positive (Version 1) to negative (Version 6) and its impact on diminishing the story's influence.
Content Engagement Metrics Prediction: Predict how the shift towards negative framing affects reader engagement and sharing behavior.
Impact on Public Discourse Analysis: Assess the potential for the increasingly negative narrative to suppress public discussion or interest in the topic.

▶ **Case Study 2: To Prompt the Story (Positive Impact)**

Sentiment Trend Analysis: Evaluate how increasing positivity (Version 6 to Version 1) amplifies the story's impact.
Audience Reception Simulation: Simulate audience responses to positive framing and measure potential uplift in engagement.
Impact on Public Discourse Analysis: Consider how a positive shift might enhance public interest and stimulate broader discourse.

▶ **Case Study 3: Simultaneous Version Release**

Information Overload Analysis: Examine how simultaneous release of multiple narratives leads to confusion and difficulty in forming a coherent opinion.

Polarity and Tone Analysis: Assess how contrasting polarities and tones in different versions contribute to information overload.

▶ **Case Study 4: Random Distribution Across Cycles**

Comparative Textual Analysis: Understand how random distribution affects the consistency of information received by the audience.
Audience Reception Simulation: Predict audience reactions to receiving randomly varied narratives over time.

▶ **Case Study 5: Alternating Positives and Negatives**

Sentiment and Polarity Fluctuation Analysis: Examine how alternating sentiments influence public mood and perceptions over time.
Content Engagement Metrics Prediction: Assess how fluctuating narratives affect reader engagement and sharing patterns.

▶ **Case Study 6: Strategic Posting with Intent**

Audience Targeting Analysis: Evaluate the effectiveness of strategic posting in shaping public opinion or redirecting focus.
Thematic Consistency and Variation Analysis: Assess how strategic intent is maintained or altered across different versions.

▶ **Case Study 7: Alignment with Current Trends**

Trend Correlation Analysis: Examine how aligning each version with current trends impacts the story's relevance and audience resonance.
Impact on Public Discourse Analysis: Analyze how trend alignment influences the narrative within public discussions and social media.

▶ **Case Study 8: Pairing with Targeted Trends or News**

Compound Effect Analysis: Investigate the effects of pairing news versions with specific trends on audience perception and engagement.
Comparative Textual Analysis: Examine how different pairings change the contextual framing of the story.

▶ **Case Study 9: Misinformation, Disinformation, Manipulation, and Propaganda**

Ethical and Societal Impact Analysis: This study delves into the ethical concerns and societal consequences of utilizing personalized news to disseminate misinformation, disinformation, and propaganda. It examines how the tailored nature of news content can potentially be exploited for manipulating public opinion, spreading false narratives, and shaping socio-political discourses in a biased manner.

Public Trust and Perception Analysis: The focus of this analysis is on assessing the long-term effects of such manipulative practices on public trust and the overall credibility of news sources. It explores how the deliberate distortion of news, under the guise of personalization, can erode public confidence in media outlets and potentially lead to a fragmented, polarized information landscape.

This comprehensive study aims to shed light on the fine line between personalization and manipulation in news media, highlighting the critical need for ethical standards and responsible use of AI technologies in news dissemination.

Each case study, when examined with these analytical lenses, provides profound insights into the multifaceted effects of news personalization. These analyses help understand the power of personalized news in shaping public perception and the potential risks associated with its misuse.

## Additional In-Depth Case Study Analysis

In the dynamic landscape of news personalization and dissemination, there exist several underexplored areas that offer rich ground for in-depth case study analysis. These additional studies are significant as they delve into the nuances of news personalization, exploring its multifaceted impacts on society, individual psychology, and the evolving media ecosystem. Each of these studies can provide profound insights into the subtleties of how news is consumed, interpreted, and internalized in the age of advanced AI technologies like 'News Oracle'. They are crucial for understanding not just the immediate effects of news personalization, but also its long-term implications for democratic discourse, cultural dynamics, and individual cognitive biases.

▶ Cognitive Bias and News Personalization: This study would investigate how personalized news content might reinforce or challenge existing cognitive biases and belief systems. It would explore the psychological implications of consuming news that aligns closely with individual viewpoints, potentially leading to echo chambers or increased polarization.

▶ Cultural and Demographic Influence on News Perception: This analysis could focus on how different cultural and demographic groups perceive and react to the same news content. It would be significant in understanding the diverse ways in which news personalization resonates with or alienates various segments of the population.

▶ Impact of Personalization on Political Discourse: An in-depth study in this area would assess how personalized news affects political engagement and discourse. It would explore whether such news personalization leads to more informed political discussions or contributes to partisanship and divisiveness.

▶ Long-term Effects on Public Knowledge and Awareness: This case study would analyze the long-term educational and informational impacts of personalized news. It would seek to understand if personalized news helps in building a more informed society or limits the breadth of public knowledge by creating informational silos.

▶ Ethical Implications of AI-Driven News Generation: This study would delve into the ethical considerations surrounding AI-generated news content, particularly focusing on issues like the transparency of sources, the potential for AI biases, and the accountability of AI-driven news platforms.

▶ Economic and Business Models in AI-Personalized News: This case study would explore the economic impacts of AI-driven news personalization, examining how it affects the business models of news organizations and the broader media industry, including advertising and content monetization strategies.

These additional in-depth case studies are vital for a comprehensive understanding of the complex interplay between AI-driven news personalization, societal dynamics, and individual behavior. They hold the key to unlocking a balanced and ethical approach to news dissemination in an AI-dominated future.

**Conclusion of In-Depth Case Study Analysis**: The completion of our in-depth analysis of the nine case studies within "News Perception in Motion: Revolutionizing News and Media with News Oracle AGI GPT" offers a rich tapestry of insights into the power and complexities of news personalization. These case studies underscore the profound influence of tailored content on public perception, ranging from subtle shifts in sentiment to significant alterations in the narrative structure. They illuminate both the potential and the pitfalls of leveraging AI-driven personalization in news dissemination, revealing how it can both enrich and distort the public dialogue.

The studies collectively demonstrate the capacity of personalized news to not only inform but also misinform, underscoring the critical need for ethical guidelines and robust analytical frameworks in this domain. They bring to the fore the delicate balance between providing targeted content that resonates with diverse audiences and maintaining the integrity and objectivity of news reporting. In conclusion, these case studies reinforce the notion that the future of news and media is intricately tied to the responsible and thoughtful application of emerging technologies. As we venture further into this new era of personalized news, it becomes imperative to navigate these waters with an acute awareness of the impact and responsibilities that come with this powerful tool.

*Presenting critical findings and future implications from data analysis, shaping the trajectory of news media.*

# Insight in Motion

## Insights from Data

In the dynamic intersection of AI-driven news personalization and media evolution, as exemplified by the 'News Oracle' platform, data transcends its traditional role to become a key driver of media innovation and transformation. Our extensive analysis, which spans across original and personalized news content, sheds light on the profound implications these advancements hold for the future of news, media, and political engagement. This exploration is rooted in a meticulous examination of the nuances that define different news versions—sentiment, polarity, subjectivity, tone, and thematic focus. Such an analysis reflects the diverse range of audience perspectives, uncovering the multi-faceted nature of news consumption and its impact.

The methodology adopted for this analysis is comprehensive and multifaceted, incorporating techniques like sentiment analysis, thematic content evaluation, and audience response interpretation. This approach enables a deeper understanding of how varied narratives shape and influence public perception, providing a window into the complex interplay between news content and audience engagement. From this detailed examination, we derive insights that are invaluable not just for news media agencies and content creators, but also for policymakers and the general public. These insights offer a strategic roadmap, guiding stakeholders through the intricate landscape of AI-driven news personalization.

At the core of our findings is the recognition of how AI, through platforms like 'News Oracle', is reshaping the very fabric of news dissemination and consumption. This transformation is not merely about technological advancement; it's about the evolution of media practices, the shifting paradigms of political discourse, and the new challenges and opportunities that emerge in a digitally interconnected world. The insights from our data underscore the potential of AI to enhance user engagement and personalization, while also highlighting the need for ethical diligence, transparency, and a commitment to diversity in news reporting. As we venture further into this era of AI-driven journalism, these insights act as guiding principles, ensuring that the progression in news media continues to serve the fundamental goals of informed public discourse and societal well-being.

## Top Insights

▶ Impact of Sentiment and Polarity on Audience Engagement: The shift in sentiment and polarity from positive (The Activists) to negative (The Critics) significantly alters audience engagement levels. Positive narratives tend to foster a sense of optimism and encourage constructive dialogue, whereas negative narratives can lead to heightened skepticism or disengagement.

▶ Influence of Subjectivity and Tone on Perceived Credibility: Highly subjective and opinionated content (as seen in The Pessimists and The Critics) can sometimes undermine the perceived credibility of the news, especially when coupled with negative tones like sadness or anger. Conversely, balanced and neutral tones tend to enhance credibility and foster trust.

▶ Echo Chamber Effect in Personalized News: The reinforcement of existing beliefs through personalized content can lead to echo chambers, limiting exposure to diverse viewpoints. This effect is particularly evident in the transition from The Realists to The Cynics, where the increasingly narrow focus amplifies specific biases.

▶ Role of Personalization in Political Polarization: Personalized news content can exacerbate political polarization, as seen in the stark contrast between narratives catered to The Activists versus The Critics. Such polarization can impact democratic discourse and the quality of public debate.

▶ Potential for Misinformation and Manipulation: As demonstrated in the case studies, particularly Case Study 9, personalized news can be a tool for misinformation and propaganda, intentionally or unintentionally distorting public perception and opinion.

▶ Economic Implications for News Agencies: The personalized approach to news content can have significant economic implications for news agencies. Tailored content can drive higher engagement and, therefore, greater revenue opportunities, but it also raises questions about journalistic integrity and the balance between profit and public service.

▶ Ethical Considerations in AI-Driven Personalization: The ethical dimensions of AI-driven news personalization, including concerns about privacy, bias, and transparency, are highlighted as critical areas for ongoing scrutiny and regulatory consideration.

▶ Adaptive Content Strategies for Diverse Audiences: The need for news agencies to develop adaptive content strategies that cater to diverse audiences without compromising on factual accuracy or ethical standards is evident. This is crucial for maintaining a well-informed and critically engaged public.

▶ Long-term Effects on Public Knowledge and Awareness: The long-term effects of personalized news on public knowledge and awareness are complex. While it can cater to individual interests and enhance engagement, there's a risk of narrowing the breadth of public understanding by focusing too narrowly on specific topics or viewpoints.

These insights collectively paint a picture of the transformative impact of AI-driven news personalization. They highlight the need for a balanced approach that leverages the benefits of personalization while mitigating its risks, ensuring that the evolution of news media continues to serve the broader goals of informed public discourse, democratic engagement, and societal well-being.

## Case Specific Insights

Drawing insights from the nine case studies, each with a unique approach to news personalization and dissemination, we gain a deeper understanding of how different strategies can impact public perception, engagement, and the overall media landscape. These case-specific insights are particularly relevant in the context of AI-driven news platforms like 'News Oracle'.

▶ **Impact of Sequential Release (Cases 1 & 2):**

Shifting from positive to negative (Case 1) or negative to positive (Case 2) narratives over time can significantly influence public sentiment towards a story. Gradually negative narratives tend to diminish audience interest and trust, while progressively positive narratives can rejuvenate interest and engagement.

▶ **Effects of Simultaneous Version Release (Case 3):**

Releasing all personalized versions simultaneously can lead to information overload, causing confusion and a diluted impact of each version. It demonstrates the importance of timing and strategic release in news dissemination.

▶ **Consequences of Random Distribution (Case 4):**

Randomly distributing different news versions across cycles creates unpredictability and may undermine the credibility of the news source. It highlights the need for consistency and coherence in news presentation.

▶ **Influencing Perception with Alternating Releases (Case 5):**

Alternating positive and negative news releases affect public perception and sentiment. This strategy can be used to balance narratives but risks being perceived as inconsistent or manipulative if not done transparently.

▶ **Strategic Posting for Influencing Opinion (Case 6):**

Intentionally posting news with specific aims, like shaping public opinion or redirecting focus, can be effective but raises ethical questions. It underscores the fine line between informed reporting and potential manipulation.

▶ **Alignment with Current Trends (Case 7):**

Aligning news versions with current trends increases relevance and engagement but may lead to reinforcing echo chambers if not balanced with diverse perspectives.

▶ **Pairing with Targeted Trends or News (Case 8):**

Strategically pairing news versions with specific trends or other news stories can amplify the impact and relevance of the content. However, this approach should be used judiciously to avoid biased or slanted reporting.

▶ **Handling Misinformation and Propaganda (Case 9):**

The potential use of personalized news for spreading misinformation or propaganda highlights the need for ethical guidelines and fact-checking mechanisms. This case underlines the responsibility of news platforms to maintain integrity and combat false information.

▶ **Ethical and Social Implications:**

Across all case studies, there is a recurring theme of the ethical and social implications of news personalization. The power to shape public opinion comes with a responsibility to uphold journalistic standards and ensure a balanced, factual representation of news.

▶ Long-term Public Trust:

The long-term impact on public trust and credibility of news sources is a critical consideration. Strategies that prioritize sensationalism or manipulation over factual reporting can erode trust over time.

These case-specific insights emphasize the complex interplay between news personalization, audience perception, and the ethical landscape of digital journalism. They highlight the potential of platforms like 'News Oracle' to revolutionize news consumption while also underscoring the importance of using these powerful tools with careful consideration of their broader societal impact.

## Overall Insights from All Case Studies

The comprehensive analysis of the nine case studies provides a holistic view of the effects of advanced news personalization techniques. These insights are especially pertinent in understanding the broader implications of AI-driven platforms like 'News Oracle' in shaping public perception and discourse. Here are the overarching insights derived from all the case studies:

▶ **Dynamic Influence on Public Perception:**

News personalization significantly influences public perception. Different strategies, whether they involve sequential release, random distribution, or strategic posting, can sway public opinion and shape the narrative around key issues.

▶ **Information Overload and Confusion:**

Simultaneous release of multiple news versions can lead to information overload, causing confusion among the audience. This underscores the importance of curating news content to avoid overwhelming the audience.

▶ **Balance between Personalization and Credibility:**

While personalization enhances engagement, there's a fine balance to be maintained to ensure credibility. Excessive personalization, especially if it borders on misinformation or manipulation, can erode trust in the news source.

▶ **Ethical Considerations in News Dissemination:**

The case studies collectively highlight the ethical considerations in the use of AI for news personalization. Ethical reporting, transparency, and accountability are paramount in maintaining the integrity of news platforms.

▶ **Potential for Echo Chambers:**

Personalized news, if not managed properly, can lead to the creation of echo chambers, where users are only exposed to news that aligns with their existing beliefs, potentially polarizing public opinion.

▶ **Strategic Use of News Personalization:**

The strategic use of news personalization to influence public opinion or trends demonstrates the powerful role of AI in shaping media narratives. However, this power must be wielded responsibly.

▶ **Impact on Public Trust:**

Long-term public trust in news media is directly impacted by the way news is personalized and disseminated. Practices that prioritize factual integrity over sensationalism are crucial in maintaining trust.

▶ **Importance of Diverse Perspectives:**

Ensuring a range of perspectives in news reporting is essential to provide a balanced view and prevent the spread of misinformation or biased reporting.

▶ **Adaptability and Responsiveness of News Platforms:**

AI-driven platforms like 'News Oracle' need to be adaptable and responsive to changing news dynamics, audience preferences, and ethical considerations.

▶ **Future of News Consumption:**

These case studies collectively point towards a future of news consumption that is increasingly personalized, interactive, and AI-driven, with a strong emphasis on ethical and responsible journalism.

In conclusion, the insights from these case studies underscore the transformative potential of AI in the news industry. They also highlight the need for a balanced approach that considers the impact on public perception, the importance of ethical reporting, and the responsibility to provide accurate and diverse news content. As AI continues to evolve, so will its role in shaping the future of news and media.

## Summary of Top Insights

Our comprehensive analysis, encompassing data-specific insights, individual case studies, and overarching observations, reveals critical trends and implications for the future of news personalization and media practices, particularly within the context of 'News Oracle'. Here's a summary of the key insights:

▶ Top Insights: The data reflects a broad spectrum of public sentiment, from highly positive to deeply negative, illustrating the diverse range of audience perspectives.

Personalization significantly alters the tone, sentiment, and focus of news articles, impacting how different audience groups perceive and react to the same news story.

▶ Data-Specific Insights: Semantic shifts in language, structure, and thematic focus are crucial in aligning news content with specific audience preferences.

The gradual change from positive to negative sentiment across different versions demonstrates the subtle yet powerful influence of language and tone in shaping audience perception.

▶ Case Specific Insights: Each case study highlights different aspects of news personalization, from strategic content release to the creation of echo chambers and the risk of misinformation.

The studies reveal how the timing and method of news release can either enhance or diminish the story's impact, indicating the strategic importance of content curation.

▶ Overall Insights from All Case Studies: The collective insights underscore the dynamic role of AI-driven news personalization in shaping public opinion and discourse.

Ethical considerations, balance in reporting, and the maintenance of public trust emerge as crucial factors in responsible news dissemination.

▶ Integrated Summary: From our extensive analysis, it's evident that news personalization, powered by AI technologies like 'News Oracle', has a profound impact on how news is consumed and perceived. The ability to tailor content to individual preferences can enhance engagement but also carries the risk of creating biased perspectives and misinformation. Ethical reporting, diversity of perspectives, and maintaining a balance between personalization and credibility are pivotal for the integrity of news media. The insights from our data and case studies emphasize the need for responsible use of AI in news personalization, ensuring that it serves to inform and educate, rather than mislead or polarize audiences. As we move forward, these insights will be invaluable in guiding the development of AI-driven news platforms to be more ethical, transparent, and inclusive.

## Comprehensive Conclusion: Synthesizing Insights from Data

After an exhaustive examination of the data, including the original news article and its six personalized versions, along with in-depth case studies, we have arrived at pivotal insights that hold profound implications for the future of media and journalism. These insights not only unravel the technical capabilities of AI in news personalization but also highlight the ethical, social, and political dimensions intertwined with this technology.

- ▶ Data Specific Insights: The manipulation of sentiment and tone in news articles can significantly sway public opinion, emphasizing the power of emotional appeal in news consumption.

  Personalization trends, such as shifts in polarity and subjectivity, highlight the delicate balance between catering to audience preferences and maintaining journalistic objectivity.

- ▶ Case Specific Insights: The strategic release of news versions, whether sequential or simultaneous, has far-reaching impacts on audience engagement and perception, underlining the importance of timing and presentation in news dissemination.

  The creation of echo chambers and the potential for misinformation underscore the ethical responsibilities in AI-driven news personalization.

- ▶ Overall Insights from All Case Studies: The insights collectively paint a picture of a future where news consumption is highly personalized, yet this personalization comes with the need for heightened ethical vigilance.

  The role of AI in potentially shaping political discourse and public opinion raises questions about the balance of power between technology providers, news agencies, and the public.

- ▶ Top Insights: The comprehensive analysis points to a transformative era in news consumption, where AI-driven personalization can enhance user engagement but also necessitates a cautious approach to avoid polarizing narratives and misinformation.

  The insights call for a collaborative effort among technologists, journalists, and policymakers to harness the benefits of AI in news while safeguarding democratic values and public trust.

In conclusion, the insights from our data provide a roadmap for the responsible integration of AI in news media. They highlight the need for a multifaceted approach that considers technological advancements, audience preferences, and ethical boundaries. As we embrace this new era of AI-driven journalism, it is imperative to navigate these waters with a commitment to transparency, diversity, and integrity, ensuring that the evolution of news media continues to serve the broader goals of informed public discourse and societal welfare.

*Exploring News Oracle's expansive influence beyond news, venturing into diverse domains and potential applications.*

# Insight in Motion

## Benefits and Risks - and Impacts

As we delve into the multifaceted world of News Oracle AGI GPT, it is essential to navigate the landscape of its potential benefits, inherent risks, and the overarching impacts it may have on the media industry and society at large. This technology, a beacon of advanced AI in the realm of news and media, brings a transformative potential that is as vast as it is complex. Our exploration will dissect these dimensions, offering a comprehensive understanding of how News Oracle AGI GPT could reshape not only how we consume news but also how we perceive and interact with the world around us.

## Benefits

The deployment of News Oracle AGI GPT in the news and media sector offers a range of advantages, from personalized content delivery to enhanced predictive analytics. These benefits not only improve user experience but also open new frontiers in information processing and content generation. The technology's ability to adapt and interact with users in a dynamic manner is set to revolutionize the traditional paradigms of news consumption.

▶ Enhanced Personalization: Offers highly tailored content, improving user engagement and satisfaction.

▶ Advanced Predictive Analysis: Capable of forecasting trends and potential future events, providing valuable insights for various sectors.

▶ Efficient Information Processing: Rapidly analyzes and synthesizes vast amounts of data, significantly improving the efficiency of information dissemination.

▶ Diverse Content Generation: Generates a wide range of content, from news articles to creative writing, catering to different audience needs.

▶ Interactive User Experience: Provides a dynamic and interactive platform for users, revolutionizing the way information is consumed and interacted with.

▶ Educational and Research Aid: Acts as a powerful tool for educational purposes and in-depth research, facilitating learning and discovery.

▶ Enhanced Accessibility: Makes complex information more accessible to a broader audience, breaking down barriers to information access.

## Risks and Challenges

Despite its numerous advantages, News Oracle AGI GPT also poses significant risks and challenges. The potential for algorithmic biases, the spread of misinformation, and privacy concerns are among the key issues that need addressing. Furthermore, the reliance on such advanced AI systems could challenge existing journalistic practices and raise ethical questions about the role of AI in news creation and distribution.

▶ Potential for Bias: AI algorithms may inadvertently perpetuate biases present in training data, leading to skewed content.

▶ Misinformation and Manipulation: There is a risk of spreading misinformation or being used for manipulative purposes, especially in sensitive political contexts.

▶ Overdependence on Technology: Reliance on AI for news generation and consumption might lead to a reduction in human editorial oversight.

▶ Privacy Concerns: Collecting and analyzing user data for personalization raises significant privacy concerns.

▶ Echo Chamber Effect: Personalized content can result in echo chambers, limiting exposure to diverse viewpoints and opinions.

▶ Erosion of Traditional Journalism: The rise of AI-generated content could challenge the role and skills of traditional journalists.

▶ Ethical and Legal Implications: The use of AI in news generation and distribution poses complex ethical and legal questions.

## Overall Impacts

The impact of News Oracle AGI GPT extends beyond the immediate realm of news and media. Its implications touch upon various facets of society, economy, and global communication. From influencing public opinion and political discourse to reshaping economic models in the media industry, the ripple effects of this technology are far-reaching. It necessitates a balanced approach, where the benefits are leveraged to foster a more informed and connected world, while vigilantly addressing the risks to maintain the integrity and trustworthiness of news media.

▶ Impact on Media Landscape: News Oracle AGI GPT has the potential to radically transform the media landscape, offering new ways of content creation and consumption but also posing challenges to traditional media models.

▶ Societal Impact: The way news is generated and consumed can significantly influence public opinion, political discourse, and societal dynamics. The platform's ability to personalize and predict can have far-reaching effects on societal behavior and attitudes.

▶ Economic Impact: For news and media agencies, the adoption of such AI technology can lead to new business models and revenue streams, though it may also disrupt existing market structures.

▶ Global Influence: On a global scale, the technology can aid in bridging information gaps between different regions, offering a more interconnected and informed world.

In essence, the journey with News Oracle AGI GPT is a path of exploration and responsibility. It invites stakeholders across the spectrum – from media professionals and technologists to policymakers and the general public – to engage in a dialogue about the future of news in our increasingly digital and AI-integrated world. While News Oracle AGI GPT offers transformative benefits, it also brings forth significant risks and challenges that must be carefully managed. Balancing the advantages with the potential negative impacts is essential to ensure that this technology serves to enhance, rather than compromise, the quality of information and public discourse in our society.

## Summary and Conclusion

The introduction of News Oracle AGI GPT into the world of news and media brings a host of benefits, including personalized content delivery, efficient data processing, and predictive insights. However, it also presents challenges such as potential biases, risks of misinformation, and a shift in the media landscape that could impact traditional journalism.

The overall impact of News Oracle AGI GPT extends far beyond technological advancement; it touches upon economic, societal, and global domains. As we embrace this technology, it's crucial to balance its benefits with potential risks. Maintaining ethical standards, ensuring accuracy, and fostering a diverse and inclusive media environment are imperative. In conclusion, while News Oracle AGI GPT offers a glimpse into the future of news and media, responsible usage and ethical considerations will dictate its role in shaping our society.

*Weighing the multifaceted benefits against potential challenges posed by News Oracle AGI GPT in news media.*

*Analyzing the broad spectrum of impacts, both positive and negative, stemming from the use of advanced AI in news generation.*

# Insight in Motion

## Ethical, Social, and Legal Considerations

In the rapidly evolving landscape of AI-driven news media, exemplified by platforms like News Oracle AGI GPT, it is critical to examine the multifaceted implications that these technologies bring to the fore. The integration of advanced AI in news generation and dissemination not only heralds a new era of information accessibility and customization but also introduces complex ethical, social, and legal challenges that must be navigated with caution and foresight. This exploration into the ethical, social, and legal considerations is aimed at ensuring the responsible and beneficial deployment of AI in the news industry.

## Ethical Considerations

Ethical issues revolve around the principles and moral values governing AI's use in news media. These encompass concerns related to bias and fairness in AI algorithms, transparency and accountability in AI-driven processes, privacy concerns arising from data collection, intellectual property rights in AI-generated content, and maintaining editorial integrity and journalistic standards.

▶ Bias and Fairness: AI algorithms, including those in News Oracle, are only as unbiased as the data they are trained on. There is a risk of perpetuating existing biases or creating new ones, which can skew news content and influence public opinion unfairly.

▶ Transparency and Accountability: The 'black box' nature of AI algorithms can lead to a lack of transparency in how news content is generated and personalized. Ensuring accountability for the content produced by AI is crucial, especially in scenarios where misinformation or contentious issues are involved.

▶ Privacy Concerns: Personalization of news content requires data on user preferences and behaviors. This raises privacy concerns, as sensitive information might be collected, stored, or potentially misused.

**71**

▶ Intellectual Property Rights: With AI generating content, questions arise about the ownership and copyright of AI-created materials. This includes determining who is responsible for the content AI produces.

▶ Editorial Integrity and Journalistic Standards: Maintaining journalistic standards and editorial integrity in an AI-driven environment is essential. There is a need to balance technological efficiency with journalistic ethics.

## Social Considerations

The social impact of AI in news media extends to its influence on public discourse, democracy, and the job landscape in the media industry. The potential for AI to create echo chambers, affect democratic processes, and transform employment patterns in journalism and media raises significant social questions that demand thorough examination and thoughtful responses.

## Legal Considerations

On the legal front, the deployment of AI in news media intersects with regulatory compliance, liability issues, the complexities of cross-border data flows, and the emergence of new legal frameworks. These considerations are vital in navigating the legal landscape, ensuring adherence to media laws, and addressing liability in AI-generated content scenarios.

▶ Impact on Public Discourse: AI-driven personalization can lead to echo chambers, where individuals are only exposed to viewpoints similar to their own, potentially polarizing public discourse.

▶ Influence on Democracy: The role of AI in shaping political news and opinions can have profound effects on democratic processes. Ensuring balanced and fair representation of political viewpoints is vital.

▶ Changing Job Landscape in Media: AI technologies can automate certain aspects of news production, which could lead to changes in the job market for journalists and other media professionals.

▶ Regulatory Compliance: Ensuring that AI-driven news platforms comply with existing media laws and regulations, including those related to misinformation, hate speech, and incitement, is essential.

▶ Liability Issues: Determining liability in cases where AI-generated content leads to harm or legal issues is complex. This might include defamation, invasion of privacy, or incitement.

▶ Cross-border Data Flow: As AI platforms operate globally, they must navigate the legal complexities of cross-border data flows and comply with diverse data protection laws.

▶ Emerging Legal Frameworks: There is a need for emerging legal frameworks that specifically address the nuances of AI in news media, balancing innovation with ethical and social responsibilities.

In conclusion, addressing these ethical, social, and legal considerations is imperative for the responsible advancement of AI technologies in news media. As AI continues to integrate into this field, continuous dialogue and collaboration among technologists, legal experts, journalists, policymakers, and the public will be key to harnessing its benefits while safeguarding democratic values and societal well-being.

*Navigating the complex ethical, social, and legal terrain shaped by AI advancements in news media.*

*Critical examination of the moral and societal implications of AI-driven news platforms, highlighting legal considerations.*

# Insight in Motion

## Misuse of Personalization Technologies

### The Perils of AI in News Media: Navigating Risks and Mitigating Misuse

In an age where AI-driven platforms like News Oracle AGI GPT are revolutionizing news media, the dawn of unprecedented opportunities is also accompanied by significant risks and potential misuses. This section delves into the intricate balance of leveraging the advancements in AI for news generation and personalization, while being acutely aware of the ethical, social, and legal implications that accompany these technologies. As we embark on this exploration, we aim to unravel the complex layers of risks associated with AI in news media, ranging from biases in personalization algorithms to the spread of misinformation, privacy concerns, and the impact on democratic discourse. Understanding these risks is crucial in developing comprehensive strategies to mitigate misuse and ensure AI's responsible and ethical application in shaping the future of news and information dissemination.

## Risks and Misuse in AI-Driven News Media

Exploring the darker side of AI in news media, this section highlights critical risks such as biases in algorithms, the spread of misinformation, and the impact on democratic discourse. It underscores the importance of recognizing these challenges to maintain the integrity and trustworthiness of news sources.

- ▶ Bias and Stereotyping in Personalization Algorithms: AI systems may inadvertently perpetuate biases, leading to stereotypical news content that lacks diversity and inclusivity.
- ▶ Spread of Misinformation and Disinformation: The ease of content creation through AI can be exploited to disseminate false or misleading information, potentially on a large scale.
- ▶ Manipulation of Public Opinion: News personalization can be misused to manipulate public opinion by selectively presenting or omitting information, thus shaping perceptions in a skewed manner.
- ▶ Echo Chambers and Polarization: Personalized news feeds might create echo chambers, reinforcing users' existing beliefs and contributing to social and political polarization.

▶ Compromise of Editorial Integrity: Over-reliance on AI for news generation may undermine journalistic standards and editorial integrity, leading to a decline in the quality of news reporting.

▶ Privacy Concerns: The data-driven nature of AI personalization raises concerns about user privacy, data security, and the potential misuse of personal information.

▶ Legal and Ethical Challenges: The automated nature of AI-generated content can lead to complex legal and ethical dilemmas, particularly regarding accountability and intellectual property rights.

▶ Impact on Democratic Discourse: The unchecked use of AI in news media can affect democratic processes, where informed decision-making is based on a diverse and balanced news landscape.

▶ Erosion of Public Trust: Misuse of AI in news generation and personalization can erode public trust in media outlets, leading to cynicism and a disengaged audience.

▶ Overdependence on AI: An overreliance on AI for news creation and distribution may reduce the role of human judgment and editorial oversight, leading to a potential decline in journalistic quality and diversity of perspectives.

## Mitigation Strategies

This section focuses on the essential countermeasures to address the risks associated with AI-driven news media. From implementing ethical guidelines to establishing robust fact-checking protocols, these strategies are crucial in ensuring responsible and trustworthy use of AI in news generation.

To counter these risks, a multifaceted approach is essential:

▶ Implementing robust ethical guidelines and transparency in AI algorithms to prevent biases.

▶ Establishing fact-checking protocols and editorial oversight to combat misinformation and disinformation.

▶ Promoting diversity and inclusivity in AI-driven content to avoid echo chambers and polarization.

▶ Upholding privacy standards and data protection laws to safeguard user information.

▶ Ensuring accountability and compliance with legal and ethical norms in AI-generated content.

In conclusion, the journey through the multifaceted risks and potential misuses of AI in news media underscores the necessity for vigilance, ethical responsibility, and strategic foresight. The insights gained from examining the perils associated with News Oracle AGI GPT and similar platforms

**75**

illuminate the path towards a more responsible and sustainable integration of AI in news media. It is evident that while AI has the potential to significantly enhance the quality and personalization of news content, it also poses risks that could undermine the integrity of news media, erode public trust, and impact societal discourse.

To navigate these challenges, a proactive approach encompassing ethical guidelines, transparency, privacy protection, and editorial oversight is imperative. The development of AI in news media should be guided by a commitment to uphold journalistic standards, promote diversity, ensure factual accuracy, and maintain a balance between innovation and ethical responsibility. It is through such concerted efforts that we can harness the transformative power of AI in news media, making it a tool for enlightenment and empowerment rather than misinformation and manipulation.

As we continue to advance in the digital era, the role of AI in news media will undoubtedly evolve. It is our collective responsibility to shape this evolution in a way that respects ethical principles, safeguards democratic values, and contributes positively to the societal discourse. The future of news media, empowered by AI, holds immense possibilities, and it is up to us to ensure that this future is built on a foundation of integrity, responsibility, and trust.

*Identifying and addressing the top risks and potential misuses of AI in the context of news and media.*

*Exploring the ethical and practical pitfalls inherent in AI-driven news, urging vigilance and responsible use.*

# Insight in Motion

## Benefits for News/Social Media Agencies

The integration of News Oracle AGI GPT into the operations of news and social media agencies heralds a transformative era in media and journalism. This advanced AI technology brings a plethora of immediate benefits and opens the door to future potentials that could redefine the landscape of news creation, distribution, and consumption. In an industry that thrives on staying ahead of the curve, the implications of such a technological leap are profound and multifaceted.

From enhancing the personalization of content to revolutionizing the efficiency of newsrooms, News Oracle AGI GPT stands at the forefront of a significant shift in how news is produced, delivered, and experienced. The technology not only streamlines operational workflows but also provides invaluable insights into audience behaviors, setting the stage for more engaging and relevant news content. Furthermore, as the technology matures, it promises even more groundbreaking advancements, including the potential for fully automated newsrooms, hyper-personalized user experiences, and ethically governed AI operations.

The immediate benefits such as efficient content generation, data-driven insights, and cost reductions are just the tip of the iceberg. Looking forward, we can anticipate developments like advanced predictive analysis, deepfake detection, and AI-driven investigative reporting that could further elevate the quality and impact of news reporting.

In essence, News Oracle AGI GPT is not just a tool for today's news and social media agencies; it is a gateway to the future of journalism, offering both immediate advantages and exciting possibilities for innovation in news media.

This section delves into the myriad benefits that News Oracle AGI GPT offers to news and social media agencies. It explores how this cutting-edge technology can revolutionize content creation, audience engagement, and operational efficiency.

## Top 10 Benefits of News Oracle AGI GPT

The implementation of News Oracle AGI GPT in news and social media agencies marks a significant advancement in the media landscape. This section delves into the top 10 benefits that this sophisticated AI technology brings to the table. These benefits range from enhanced content accuracy and diversity to improved audience engagement and operational efficiency. By exploring these key advantages, we gain a comprehensive understanding of how News Oracle AGI GPT is not only revolutionizing current media practices but also setting a new standard for the future of news and journalism.

▶ Enhanced Personalization (Immediate): AI-driven algorithms allow for highly personalized content, catering to individual user preferences and interests.
▶ Efficient Content Generation (Immediate): Rapid creation of diverse news content, significantly reducing the time and resources needed for content production.
▶ Data-Driven Insights (Immediate): Access to real-time analytics and user data, aiding in strategic decision-making and content optimization.
▶ Increased User Engagement (Near Future): Personalization and relevant content delivery lead to higher user engagement and retention.
▶ Cost Reduction (Immediate): Automation of content generation and curation processes reduces operational costs.
▶ Real-Time Trend Tracking (Immediate): Ability to quickly identify and respond to emerging news trends and user interests.
▶ Enhanced Editorial Capabilities (Near Future): AI assistance in editorial tasks, improving efficiency and accuracy.
▶ Global Reach (Immediate): Ability to generate and curate content for a global audience, transcending language barriers.
▶ Improved Ad Targeting (Immediate): Enhanced user profiling capabilities for more effective and targeted advertising.
▶ Ethical and Balanced Reporting (Future): Potential for AI to aid in unbiased and fact-based news reporting.

## Top 10 Futuristic Potentials of News Oracle AGI GPT

As we venture into the future of AI in news media, it is exciting to contemplate the evolving capabilities and potential applications of News Oracle AGI GPT. This section highlights the top 10 futuristic potentials of this groundbreaking technology. These potentials envision a future where news generation, audience interaction, and content personalization reach unprecedented levels of sophistication and effectiveness. From predictive analytics to immersive storytelling, these futuristic potentials suggest a transformative impact of News Oracle AGI GPT on the way news will be consumed and experienced in the years to come.

- ▶ Advanced Predictive Analysis (Future): Predicting news trends and public interests with greater accuracy for proactive content strategy.
- ▶ Fully Automated Newsrooms (Far Future): Complete automation in news content creation and curation, requiring minimal human intervention.
- ▶ Deepfake Detection (Near Future): Advanced capabilities to identify and flag deepfake content and misinformation.
- ▶ Hyper-Personalized User Experiences (Near Future): Tailoring content not just to general preferences but to specific user moods and contexts.
- ▶ AI-Generated Investigative Reporting (Future): Utilizing AI for in-depth investigative journalism, uncovering insights hidden in large data sets.
- ▶ Interactive and Immersive Content (Near Future): Creating highly interactive and immersive news experiences through AR/VR integration.
- ▶ AI as News Anchors (Future): AI-powered virtual anchors providing personalized news broadcasts.
- ▶ Emotionally Intelligent Content (Future): AI that understands and adapts content based on the emotional responses of users.
- ▶ AI-Driven Crisis Management (Near Future): Utilizing AI for rapid and effective news dissemination during crises, ensuring accurate and timely information.
- ▶ Ethical AI Governance (Future): Establishing frameworks for ethical AI use in news generation, ensuring accountability and transparency.

These benefits and futuristic potentials highlight the transformative impact of News Oracle AGI GPT in reshaping the landscape of news and social media agencies. From immediate practical advantages to far-reaching future possibilities, the integration of AI technology promises a new era of news media innovation.

## Comprehensive Conclusion: Embracing the AI-Driven Future in News Media

As we delve into the benefits and futuristic potentials of News Oracle AGI GPT for news and social media agencies, it becomes clear that we are standing on the cusp of a new era in journalism and media. The immediate advantages brought forth by this technology are already reshaping the dynamics of news production and distribution, offering enhanced personalization, improved operational efficiency, and deeper audience engagement. These benefits represent a significant leap forward in meeting the evolving demands of the digital age.

Looking beyond the immediate, the future potentials of News Oracle AGI GPT paint a picture of a more connected, responsive, and innovative news media landscape. The prospects of AI-driven predictive analysis, immersive content experiences, and ethical AI governance highlight a future where technology and journalism converge in exciting and responsible ways. These advancements promise not only to enhance the capabilities of news and social media agencies but also to enrich the overall experience for audiences worldwide.

As we embrace this AI-driven future, it is crucial to navigate the path with a keen awareness of the ethical, social, and legal implications. The journey ahead is filled with opportunities for groundbreaking innovation, but it also calls for a balanced approach that respects ethical standards and prioritizes the integrity of journalism. In this new era, News Oracle AGI GPT stands as a beacon of potential, guiding the way towards a more informed, engaged, and technologically empowered world of news media.

*Unveiling the array of benefits and futuristic potentials that News Oracle AGI GPT offers to news and social media agencies.*

*Forecasting the expanding horizons for news and social media outlets in the wake of AI advancements.*

# Insight in Motion

## What's Next and Futurist View

As we stand at the precipice of technological advancements in the realm of news media, the "What's Next and Futurist View" section aims to shed light on the potential future trends and developments in the fields of News Oracle, AGI, and ChatGPT. This forward-looking perspective is critical in understanding how these technologies will shape the future of news media, social media, and political discourse. Here, we will explore predictions and emerging trends, considering how the integration of advanced AI technologies like AGI and ChatGPT with platforms like News Oracle could revolutionize the way information is disseminated and consumed. This section not only anticipates future technological advancements but also reflects on the broader implications these innovations may have on society, media ethics, and the political landscape.

## Futurist Predictions and Trends

As we delve into the future of news and media, it is essential to explore the burgeoning trends and predictions that could redefine the landscape of journalism, social media, and political communication. In the context of News Oracle, AGI, and ChatGPT, we stand at the forefront of a revolutionary shift, where the boundaries of current technology are continuously expanded. The "Futurist Predictions and Trends" section aims to unravel these potential developments, offering insights into how these advanced technologies might evolve and the profound impact they could have on the way we consume, interact with, and understand news and information. This segment paints a picture of a future where AI is not just a tool but a transformative force, potentially reshaping every facet of news media and creating new paradigms for global communication and engagement.

- ▶ AI-Driven Personalized News Ecosystems: Future news platforms may evolve into highly sophisticated ecosystems that offer hyper-personalized content, tailored not just to individual interests but also to mood, context, and even cognitive styles.
- ▶ Emergence of Interactive and Immersive Journalism: Advancements in virtual and augmented reality, combined with AGI and ChatGPT, could lead to more immersive and interactive forms of journalism, where audiences can experience news stories in a more engaging and empathetic manner.

▶ Predictive Analytics in News Reporting: With the integration of predictive analytics, news platforms like News Oracle could provide anticipatory news coverage, offering insights into potential future events and trends based on real-time data analysis.

▶ Automated Fact-Checking and Verification: As misinformation remains a significant challenge, future iterations of AGI and ChatGPT could include advanced, real-time fact-checking capabilities, significantly enhancing the credibility and reliability of news content.

▶ Enhanced Audience Engagement Through Conversational AI: The fusion of ChatGPT's conversational AI with news platforms will likely lead to more interactive and engaging news experiences, where audiences can have personalized dialogues with their news content.

▶ AI as a Tool for Unbiased Reporting: Future developments in AI could focus on eliminating biases in news reporting, striving for a more balanced and equitable presentation of news.

▶ Real-Time Global News Translation and Localization: News Oracle may offer real-time translation and localization features, breaking down language barriers and bringing global news to diverse audiences in their native languages.

▶ Integration with Social Media Dynamics: AI-driven news platforms could become more intricately integrated with social media, utilizing user-generated content and social trends to enrich news reporting and analysis.

▶ Ethical AI Governance in News Media: The future will likely see the establishment of more robust ethical frameworks and governance models for AI in journalism, addressing concerns around privacy, bias, and transparency.

▶ AI in Political Campaigns and Public Policy: The use of AI for analyzing public opinion and shaping political campaigns could become more sophisticated, potentially impacting democratic processes and public policy development.

## Conclusion: Navigating the Future Landscape

The future of news media, shaped by technologies like News Oracle, AGI, and ChatGPT, promises a landscape that is more dynamic, interactive, and personalized. However, navigating this future will require a careful balance between embracing technological innovation and addressing the ethical, social, and legal challenges that arise. As we venture into this new era, the focus will be on harnessing the potential of AI to enhance the quality of journalism and public discourse, while vigilantly safeguarding the principles of unbiased reporting, transparency, and trust. The vision of the future, thus, is not just about technological advancement but also about fostering a more informed, engaged, and connected global society.

### *Speculating on the future trajectory of news and media in the context of advancing AI technologies.*

# Insight in Motion

## Conclusion

### Synthesizing the Future of News Media with News Oracle AGI GPT

As we conclude this comprehensive exploration of the News Oracle AGI GPT and its monumental impact on news media, politics, and social discourse, it becomes clear that we are witnessing a paradigm shift in information dissemination and consumption. This article has traversed a wide array of topics, each contributing to a nuanced understanding of how AI-driven personalization is reshaping the news industry. Let us reflect on the key takeaways and the profound implications they hold for our future.

### Reflecting on the Journey: Overview and Insights

As we encapsulate the extensive exploration of "News Perception in Motion Empowered by News Oracle," it is imperative to revisit the key sections that have paved our understanding of this revolutionary technology. This comprehensive article has traversed through various facets of AI-driven news personalization, dissecting the intricate layers of how News Oracle AGI GPT is reshaping the landscape of news, media, and societal discourse. Below is a concise introduction to each pivotal section and the top findings that emerged from our journey. These reflections serve not just as a summary but as critical touchpoints that echo the transformative influence and future potential of this groundbreaking technology.

### Overview of Key Sections

We embarked on a journey through the evolving terrain of news media, marking each milestone with in-depth analysis and critical insights. From the historical roots of digital news evolution to the futuristic vistas opened by AI, every section has contributed to a comprehensive understanding of the seismic shifts in news media.

▶ Background and Emergence of AI in News: We began by setting the stage with the historical evolution of news in the digital age, emphasizing how AI technologies like AGI and GPT have revolutionized news creation and consumption.

▶ Technical Foundations of News Oracle AGI GPT: Delving into the mechanics, we explored the sophistication of AGI, the linguistic prowess of GPT, and the seamless integration of these technologies in News Oracle, paving the way for a new era of personalized news.

▶ Methods and Techniques in AI-Driven News: This section highlighted the innovative techniques in news personalization, content creation, and predictive forecasting, demonstrating the capabilities of AI in curating bespoke news experiences.

▶ Data Overview and Personalization Trends: We presented an in-depth analysis of personalized news versions, revealing how variations in sentiment, tone, and subjectivity/objectivity can dramatically alter audience perception.

▶ Insightful Case Studies: Through nine meticulous case studies, we examined various strategies in news personalization, uncovering the multifaceted impacts these have on public discourse and perception.

▶ Wider Applications Beyond News and Politics: The versatility of News Oracle AGI GPT extends beyond news, offering potential applications in various fields, each presenting unique benefits and challenges.

▶ Benefits, Risks, and Impact Analysis: We weighed the advantages of News Oracle AGI GPT against potential challenges, underlining the need for a balanced approach in leveraging this technology.

▶ Ethical, Social, and Legal Considerations: This crucial segment addressed the moral, societal, and legal implications of AI in news media, emphasizing the importance of ethical standards and legal frameworks.

▶ Risks and Misuse in AI-Driven News Media: We discussed potential misuses and risks, from spreading misinformation to creating echo chambers, underscoring the need for responsible usage of AI in news media.

▶ Advantages for News and Social Media Agencies: Highlighting the benefits for news and social media outlets, we explored how News Oracle AGI GPT can enhance content quality, audience engagement, and operational efficiency.

▶ What's Next and Futurist View: We projected into the future, speculating on emerging trends and potential developments in AI-driven news, shaping our expectations of what lies ahead in this rapidly evolving field.

## Top 10 Findings and Provocative Thoughts

The culmination of our exploration into News Oracle AGI GPT and its multifaceted implications has yielded profound findings and stimulating thoughts. These key insights, outlined as the top 10 findings, encapsulate the essence of our study and project forward-thinking perspectives on the future of news media in the AI era.

Let's delve into these summaries, each a microcosm of the larger narrative, offering a deeper grasp of the dynamic world of AI-driven news personalization and its far-reaching impacts.

- ▶ The Power of Personalization: News Oracle AGI GPT demonstrates how AI-driven personalization can revolutionize news consumption, making it more relevant, engaging, and insightful for individual users.
- ▶ Balancing AI with Human Oversight: While AI offers remarkable capabilities, the importance of human judgment and editorial oversight remains paramount to ensure quality and ethical standards.
- ▶ Potential for Echo Chambers: The personalization of news content risks creating echo chambers, highlighting the need for exposing audiences to diverse perspectives.
- ▶ Ethical Implications: The ethical dimensions of AI in news - from privacy concerns to bias and accountability - call for robust ethical frameworks and transparency in AI algorithms.
- ▶ AI as a Double-Edged Sword: While AI can enhance news quality and engagement, it also poses risks like misinformation and manipulation, demanding vigilant checks and balances.
- ▶ Democratizing News Creation: News Oracle AGI GPT has the potential to democratize news creation, allowing more voices and perspectives to be heard, thereby enriching public discourse.
- ▶ Reshaping Political Discourse: The technology's impact on political news and discourse can be profound, influencing public opinion and democratic processes.
- ▶ Future of AI in Journalism: As AI technologies continue to evolve, their role in journalism is set to become more prominent, reshaping the profession in unforeseen ways.
- ▶ Global Impact on Society and Culture: The widespread adoption of AI-driven news platforms like News Oracle will have far-reaching effects on global society and culture, influencing how we perceive and interact with the world.
- ▶ Continued Evolution and Innovation: The future of AI in news and media is a journey of continuous evolution and innovation, promising to unveil new possibilities and challenges.

In summary, the integration of AGI and GPT in platforms like News Oracle marks a watershed moment in news media. As we embrace this new era, it is crucial to navigate these waters with a keen awareness of the potential and pitfalls, ensuring that the future of news media is not only technologically advanced but also ethically sound, socially responsible, and beneficial to the global community. The insights and discussions presented in this article serve as a foundation for this journey, sparking dialogue, debate, and development in the fascinating intersection of AI, news, and society.

*A comprehensive summation of the key findings, offering final thoughts on the future of AI in news and media.*

*Wrapping up the extensive exploration of News Oracle, the article reflects on the profound implications for news consumption and media evolution.*

**86**

# Insight in Motion

## Roadmap for Future Research

### Charting the Path Forward

As we conclude our exploration titled "News Perception in Motion Empowered by News Oracle," we find ourselves at a critical crossroads in the convergence of artificial intelligence and media. This comprehensive journey into the realm of AI, particularly through the lens of News Oracle AGI GPT, represents just the beginning of our understanding of AI's expansive potential to revolutionize news and media. Throughout this exploration, we've delved into the complex layers of AI-driven news personalization, uncovering a plethora of insights, challenges, and possibilities that set the stage for future research. This roadmap we present is not simply a collection of potential research areas; it embodies a vision for the future - a future where AI's integration into news and media significantly contributes to societal progress and adheres to ethical standards.

Moving forward, we must acknowledge that our findings from the use of News Oracle AGI GPT are foundational steps into a much larger and intricate world where technology, society, and information are in constant interplay and evolution. This section is dedicated to outlining a comprehensive path for future research endeavors. It serves as a strategic guide to traverse the ever-changing landscape of AI in news media. Our goal is to identify and address the emerging challenges and to seize opportunities that promote a more informed, ethical, and globally connected community. Each proposed direction for future research plays an essential role in a broader narrative. In this narrative, AI not only transforms our media consumption habits but also profoundly enhances our collective understanding and engagement with the world. Through this roadmap, we aim to illuminate the path for continued innovation and responsible application of AI in news media, fostering a future that is informed, ethical, and deeply connected.

## Future Research Directions

As we delve into the expansive possibilities of AI in the realms of news and media, we recognize the imperative need for continuous exploration and innovation. The integration of advanced technologies like News Oracle AGI GPT in news generation and dissemination brings forth both challenges and opportunities that warrant in-depth study and understanding. The following key research directions represent critical areas where focused investigation can significantly enrich our comprehension and application of AI in news media. These directions are not only about refining current methodologies but also about exploring new frontiers, ensuring that the evolution of AI in news media aligns with ethical standards, enhances public discourse, and adapts to the ever-changing technological landscape.

- ▶ Evolving AI Algorithms: Continuous research into the development of more sophisticated AI algorithms will be vital. This includes enhancing the accuracy, fairness, and ethical considerations in AI-driven content generation.
- ▶ Impact Assessment: Longitudinal studies to assess the long-term impact of AI-personalized news on public opinion, societal discourse, and democratic processes.
- ▶ Audience Behavioral Studies: In-depth analysis of audience behavior and engagement patterns in response to AI-personalized news content.
- ▶ Data Privacy and Security: Research focused on ensuring data privacy and security in the context of AI-driven news, addressing concerns around user data handling and consent.
- ▶ Algorithmic Transparency and Accountability: Studies exploring ways to increase transparency and accountability in news personalization algorithms.
- ▶ Cross-Cultural and Global Impact: Research into the global impact of AI in news, including cross-cultural studies to understand how different regions and cultures interact with and are influenced by AI-personalized news.
- ▶ Ethical and Legal Frameworks: Developing comprehensive ethical guidelines and legal frameworks to govern the use of AI in news media.
- ▶ Combating Misinformation: Strategies and technologies to combat the spread of misinformation and disinformation in AI-driven news platforms.
- ▶ Economic Models: Analysis of the economic implications for news agencies and the media industry as a whole, in the context of shifting towards AI-driven news generation.
- ▶ Technological Integration: Exploring the integration of emerging technologies like augmented reality, virtual reality, and blockchain with AI in news media.
- ▶ Interdisciplinary Collaboration: Encouraging interdisciplinary collaboration between computer scientists, journalists, ethicists, and legal experts to holistically approach the challenges and opportunities presented by AI in news media.
- ▶ User-Centric Design: Focusing on user-centric design approaches to make AI-driven news platforms more accessible, intuitive, and responsive to diverse audience needs.
- ▶ Social and Psychological Impacts: Investigating the social and psychological impacts of personalized news consumption, particularly in terms of mental health and well-being.
- ▶ Future Technologies: Keeping a close watch on emerging technologies and their potential applications in news media, to stay ahead of the curve in a rapidly evolving landscape.

## Concluding Thought

The roadmap for future research in AI-driven news media is expansive and dynamic, reflecting the rapidly evolving nature of technology and its societal impacts. As we forge ahead, it is imperative to approach these research endeavors with a commitment to ethical principles, inclusivity, and a vision that aligns technological advancement with the greater good of society. The journey into the future of news media, powered by AI, is one of continuous learning, adaptation, and responsible innovation.

*Outlining potential research directions and themes in the ever-evolving field of AI, news, and media.*

*"Proposing a forward-looking agenda for future exploration and study in the realm of AI-driven news personalization.*

# Insight in Motion

## Mental Health

## Understanding the Impact on Mental Health

The advent of AI-driven news personalization, as exemplified by News Oracle, brings significant implications for mental health. This section explores the psychological effects of continuous and personalized news consumption.

▶ Information Overload and Anxiety
Continuous News Stream: The relentless flow of news, personalized to individual preferences, can lead to information overload. This constant exposure, particularly to negative or sensationalized news, heightens stress and anxiety.
Managing Information Flow: Implementing features that moderate the intensity and frequency of news delivery can help manage anxiety levels.

▶ Echo Chambers and Mental Well-being
Reinforced Beliefs: Personalized news feeds can create echo chambers, reinforcing existing beliefs and biases. This insulation from diverse perspectives can diminish emotional resilience and skew worldviews.
Breaking Echo Chambers: Incorporating algorithms that introduce diverse viewpoints can help break echo chambers, fostering emotional resilience and a balanced perspective.

▶ The Role of Negative News in Mental Health
Impact of Negativity: Exposure to negative news, especially when tailored to individual fears, can significantly affect mood and exacerbate feelings of despair.
Balancing News Content: Strategies to balance news feeds with positive or uplifting stories can counteract the negative psychological impact.

## Leveraging Technology for Mental Wellness

Despite the challenges, News Oracle can play a positive role in promoting mental health:

▶ Mindful Curation of News Content
Positive Story Integration: Including positive news stories can mitigate the effects of negative news, fostering hope and resilience.

▶ Promoting Mental Health Awareness
Resource Dissemination: Utilizing the platform to spread information about mental health resources and coping strategies can increase access to support.

▶ Encouraging Healthy News Consumption Habits
Consumption Management: Features like screen-time reminders and content filters can promote healthier consumption habits, reducing stress and anxiety.

▶ Providing Diverse Perspectives
Balanced Viewpoints: Ensuring a mix of diverse viewpoints can break echo chambers and promote emotional resilience.

▶ Emphasizing Constructive Journalism
Solution-Oriented Reporting: Focusing on constructive journalism can create a more positive news experience, emphasizing hope and potential solutions.

## Addressing the Risks

Recognizing and mitigating potential risks is crucial in the context of mental health:

▶ Ensuring Ethical Personalization
Balanced Personalization: Personalization should be ethical, avoiding overly negative content and ensuring diversity in news.

▶ Transparent Algorithms
Algorithmic Clarity: Transparency in personalization algorithms can reduce the creation of harmful echo chambers.

91

▶ Regular Mental Health Check-Ins
Emotional Self-Assessment: Features that prompt regular mental health assessments can help users monitor their emotional state and encourage breaks when needed.

▶ Collaborations with Mental Health Experts
Expert Input: Involving mental health professionals in AI algorithm design can ensure that mental well-being is prioritized.

▶ Educational Content on Media Literacy
Media Literacy Resources: Offering resources on media literacy can empower users to critically analyze news, reducing the impact of sensationalism and misinformation.

**Concluding Thoughts:** As we embrace the advancements in AI and its integration into news media, it's imperative to keep the human element at the forefront, particularly concerning mental health. The potential of News Oracle AGI GPT extends beyond just transforming how we consume news; it presents an opportunity to reshape our relationship with information in a way that supports and nurtures our mental well-being. This special section not only highlights the challenges but also the transformative possibilities of AI in fostering a more mindful, informed, and mentally resilient society.

## Mental Health: Insights from the Case Studies of News Oracle

In light of the comprehensive case studies explored in "News Perception in Motion Empowered by News Oracle," this expanded special section delves deeper into the mental health implications of AI-driven news personalization and dissemination strategies. These insights draw from the diverse scenarios and outcomes presented in the case studies, providing a more nuanced understanding of how News Oracle's capabilities might influence mental well-being.

**Mental Health Insights from Individual Case Studies**

▶ **Sequential Release of News (Cases 1 & 2):**
Emotional Impact: The gradual shift from positive to negative narratives (Case 1) or vice versa (Case 2) can create emotional turbulence, impacting mental stability. Continuous exposure to increasingly negative news can heighten anxiety and pessimism, while a shift to positive news might help in restoring balance and hope.

Coping Strategies: Incorporating features that allow users to moderate the intensity of news narratives over time could help in managing emotional responses effectively.

▶ **Simultaneous Version Release (Case 3):**

Information Overload: Releasing multiple personalized versions at once can overwhelm users, leading to stress and decision fatigue.

Mindful Consumption: Integrating tools that help users filter and prioritize news based on their mental and emotional capacity can aid in reducing overload.

▶ **Random Distribution Across Cycles (Case 4):**

Uncertainty and Confusion: The unpredictability in news delivery can create a sense of confusion and insecurity, impacting mental clarity and focus.

Structured News Experience: Offering options for more structured and predictable news updates can provide a sense of control and stability to users.

▶ **Alternating Positives and Negatives (Case 5):**

Emotional Rollercoaster: Alternating between positive and negative news can lead to an emotional rollercoaster, affecting mood stability.

Balanced Reporting: Encouraging a balanced approach in news delivery, with a mix of uplifting and challenging stories, can help maintain emotional equilibrium.

▶ **Strategic Posting with Intent (Case 6):**

Manipulation Concerns: Intentional manipulation of news for specific agendas can lead to mistrust and cynicism, impacting mental health.

Transparency and Ethics: Upholding ethical standards in news presentation and maintaining transparency about the intent behind news stories can foster trust and mental well-being.

▶ **Alignment with Current Trends (Case 7):**

Echo Chamber Effect: Aligning news with current trends might reinforce existing beliefs, limiting exposure to diverse perspectives and potentially contributing to narrow-mindedness and intolerance.

Diverse Content: Ensuring diversity in news content to expose users to a range of perspectives can enhance mental flexibility and empathy.

▶ **Pairing with Targeted Trends or News (Case 8):**

Selective Exposure: This strategy might lead to selective exposure to certain types of news, possibly skewing worldviews and contributing to anxiety or paranoia.

**93**

Holistic News Presentation: Presenting news in a more holistic manner, covering a wide spectrum of topics, can provide a more balanced and less distressing news experience.

▶ **Misinformation, Disinformation, Manipulation, and Propaganda (Case 9):**
Impact on Mental Health: The spread of misinformation can create fear, anger, and helplessness, severely impacting mental health.
Fact-Checking and Verification: Incorporating robust fact-checking mechanisms and promoting news literacy can help mitigate the harmful effects of misinformation on mental health.

**Overall Mental Health Considerations: Personalization vs. Mental Health:** While personalization in news can enhance relevance, it's essential to balance it with mental health considerations. This includes providing options for users to control the level of personalization and the nature of content they receive.

▶ **Crisis Support and Resources:** Incorporating features that offer support and resources during times of crisis or heightened stress can be crucial. This might include links to mental health resources or tools for emotional self-assessment.
▶ **User Empowerment:** Empowering users with the ability to understand and manage their news consumption habits can contribute to better mental health outcomes. Features that promote mindful news consumption and provide insights into usage patterns can be beneficial.
▶ **Community Building:** Leveraging the platform to build supportive communities around shared interests or concerns can provide a sense of belonging and support, countering feelings of isolation or anxiety that can arise from negative news content.

**Conclusion:** The intersection of AI-driven news personalization and mental health is complex and multifaceted. As exemplified by the case studies of News Oracle, it is clear that while the technology holds immense potential for enhancing the news experience, it also poses significant challenges for mental health. It is imperative for platforms like News Oracle to not only focus on delivering personalized content but also to consider the psychological impact of their services, ensuring that they contribute positively to the mental

## Conclusion for Section: Special Section- Mental Health

In summary, while News Oracle's AI-driven news personalization presents challenges for mental health, there are substantial opportunities to leverage this technology for promoting mental well-being. By balancing personalization with ethical considerations, providing diverse content, and promoting healthy consumption habits, News Oracle can contribute positively to users' mental health and overall well-being.

*A dedicated exploration of the impact of News Oracle and news personalization on mental health, offering insights and strategies.*

*The special section on mental health discusses the psychological impact of AI-driven news, offering strategies for promoting mental wellness.*

*Delving into mental health, the article explores how News Oracle influences psychological well-being, from echo chambers to mindful news consumption.*

95

# Comprehensive Step-By-Step Analysis

## Walkthrough: Data, Analysis, Insights, and Case Studies

# Walkthrough

## Original News and Analysis

### Original Source of News and Short Analysis:

Title: News Headline: US Plans to Station Nuclear Weapons at RAF Lakenheath, UK in Response to Russia."

https://news.sky.com/story/us-plan-for-nuclear-weapons-to-be-stationed-at-raf-lakenheath-base-in-suffolk-13057390

Based on the recent reports, the United States is reportedly planning to station nuclear weapons at RAF Lakenheath in Suffolk, UK, marking the first time since 2008 that such weapons would be located in the UK. This move is seen as a response to the growing threat from Russia and is part of a broader NATO strategy to enhance and update nuclear sites in the wake of Russia's invasion of Ukraine. The nuclear weapons to be stationed are believed to be B61-12 gravity bombs, which can be deployed from fighter jets and are said to be three times the strength of the Hiroshima bomb.

This development has significant implications and warrants a multifaceted analysis:

1. Historical Context Analysis: This would involve looking at the history of US-UK military cooperation, the historical context of nuclear weapon stationing, and previous responses to geopolitical tensions with Russia.
2. Future Forecasting: Predicting potential diplomatic, military, and geopolitical developments that could arise from this decision.
3. News Clustering: Grouping this headline with other recent news about NATO, nuclear policies, and US-Russia relations to identify broader patterns.
4. Demographic Group Analysis: Assessing how different age groups, nationalities, and political affiliations perceive this decision.
5. Political and Social Group Analysis: Understanding the implications for various political groups, such as arms control advocates, defense hawks, and international peace organizations.
6. News/Media Perspective Analysis: Evaluating how different media outlets with varying political leanings report this news, from conservative to liberal, Western to Russian perspectives.
7. Semantic Analysis: Analyzing the language used in the headline for implications, connotations, and underlying messages.

8.  Authenticity Verification: Verifying the authenticity of the report, especially considering the sensitive nature of nuclear weapon deployment.
9.  Advertising Influence Analysis: Assessing if commercial interests, such as defense contracting, might influence the reporting.
10. Machine Generation Assessment: Identifying if the report follows standard human journalistic practices or if it shows signs of being algorithmically generated.
11. Social Media Analysis: Evaluating public opinion and discourse on social media platforms regarding the deployment of nuclear weapons.
12. Bias Detection: Identifying biases in how different media outlets might report this news, based on their editorial policies or national affiliations.
13. Sentiment Analysis: Gauging public sentiment about the decision, which could range from fear and concern to approval and support.
14. Comparative Media Analysis: Comparing coverage across various national and international news outlets.
15. Impact Analysis: Assessing the potential impact of this decision on international relations, national security, and global nuclear policy.
16. Source Credibility Assessment: Evaluating the reliability of the sources reporting this news.
17. Reader Engagement Analysis: Analyzing reader reactions, comments, and engagement with the news.
18. Visual Media Analysis: Examining any accompanying images or videos for how they represent the story.
19. Legal and Ethical Analysis: Considering the legal and ethical implications of stationing nuclear weapons, particularly under international law and treaties.
20. Global Perspective Analysis: Analyzing how this decision is viewed and impacts various regions globally, especially considering NATO and non-NATO countries.

## Original Source of News and Short Analysis:

Title: News Headline: US Plans to Station Nuclear Weapons at RAF Lakenheath, UK in Response to Russia."

https://news.sky.com/story/us-plan-for-nuclear-weapons-to-be-stationed-at-raf-lakenheath-base-in-suffolk-13057390

Headline News: US 'planning to move nuclear weapons to Suffolk RAF base'

Amid calls to ramp up preparations for a potential war between Russia and NATO forces, the US is said to be planning to move nuclear weapons to the UK for the first time since 2008. The UK's Ministry of Defence said it would neither confirm nor deny the report.

Saturday 27 January 2024 10:54, UK
News Headline: The US is reportedly planning to move nuclear warheads to the UK in response to the growing threat from Russia.

Senior figures on both sides of the Atlantic have called for preparations to be ramped up in case of a potential war between NATO forces and Russia.
To reinforce the alliance, the Telegraph reports Pentagon documents reveal the nuclear weapons will be stationed at RAF Lakenheath in Suffolk.

They are said to be three times the strength of the Hiroshima bomb.
Responding to the report, a spokesperson for the UK's Ministry of Defence said: "It remains a longstanding UK and NATO policy to neither confirm nor deny the presence of nuclear weapons at a given location."
US nuclear missiles were last held in the UK as recently as 2008, when they were removed as the Cold War threat from Russia had shrunk.
The nuclear weapons that could be located at the base are believed to be B61-12 gravity bombs, which can be deployed from fighter jets.

It's part of a NATO programme to "develop and upgrade nuclear sites" in the wake of Russia's invasion of Ukraine, the Telegraph reports.

An anti-nuclear protest outside RAF Lakenheath in 2016 (image)
Earlier this week, General Sir Patrick Sanders, the outgoing head of the British Army, said its 74,000-strong ranks need to be bolstered by at least 45,000 reservists and citizens.
General Sir Richard Sherriff, ex-deputy supreme allied commander of NATO, told Sky News the UK defence budget is not big enough to expand the armed forces alone.
He added it's time to "think the unthinkable" and consider introducing conscription to ready the country for a potential land war.
"I think we need to go further and look carefully at conscription," he said.
But Downing Street moved to rule out any plans for conscription, saying that Army service will remain voluntary.

## Top 10 News Headline

Here are the top 10 news headlines from the past two days regarding the U.S. plan to station nuclear weapons at RAF Lakenheath, UK, in response to Russia:

1. "US 'planning to move nuclear weapons to Suffolk RAF base'" 【183†source】.
2. "US nuclear weapons to be stationed in UK for first time in 15 years as fears grow over the prospect of a third world war with Vladimir Putin's Russia" 【185†source】.
3. "US nuclear weapons could be stationed in UK for first time" 【186†source】.
4. "General Sir Patrick Sanders, outgoing head of the British Army, floated the idea of a 'citizen army' to combat the threat" 【187†source】.
5. "Ukraine war latest: US to station nuclear weapons in Britain" 【188†source】.
6. "Putin 'is not going to stop with Ukraine', ex-NATO chief warns" 【189†source】.
7. "US could station nuclear weapons in UK for first time in 15 years amid growing threat from Russia" 【190†source】.
8. "RAF Lakenheath in Suffolk would be home to warheads with three times the power of the Hiroshima bomb" 【191†source】.
9. "US to store nuclear weapons in new RAF facility as NATO countries respond to Russian threat" 【192†source】.
10. "The Telegraph reports that Pentagon documents reveal plans for the stationing of nuclear weapons at RAF Lakenheath".

These headlines provide a comprehensive view of the recent developments and responses to the decision to station nuclear weapons in the UK in response to Russia.

## Initial Analysis

Based on the recent reports, the United States is reportedly planning to station nuclear weapons at RAF Lakenheath in Suffolk, UK, marking the first time since 2008 that such weapons would be located in the UK. This move is seen as a response to the growing threat from Russia and is part of a broader NATO strategy to enhance and update nuclear sites in the wake of Russia's invasion of Ukraine. The nuclear weapons to be stationed are believed to be B61-12 gravity bombs, which can be deployed from fighter jets and are said to be three times the strength of the Hiroshima bomb.

This development has significant implications and warrants a multifaceted analysis:

**100**

1. Historical Context: The last time the US stationed nuclear missiles in the UK was in 2008, during a period of reduced Cold War tensions with Russia.
2. Future Implications: This move could lead to heightened tensions between NATO and Russia, potentially affecting global diplomatic relations and security strategies.
3. News Clustering: This headline falls into a broader category of news concerning NATO-Russia relations, military strategies, and nuclear policies.
4. Demographic Analysis: Different demographic groups might have varied perceptions of this development, influenced by factors like age, location, political beliefs, and historical knowledge.
5. Political and Social Analysis: Various political and social groups, ranging from anti-nuclear activists to defense hawks, will likely have strong opinions on this decision.
6. Media Perspective: Different media outlets, depending on their political leanings and national affiliations, may portray this news differently.
7. Semantic Analysis: The language used in reporting this news can influence public perception - terms like "threat," "defense," and "security" can have significant connotations.
8. Authenticity Verification: Given the sensitive nature of the topic, it's crucial to verify the authenticity of the reports and the sources providing this information.
9. Social Media Response: The reaction on social media platforms could range from concern about escalating military tensions to debates over nuclear policy.
10. Bias Detection: Identifying potential biases in the coverage of this news is crucial, as it could influence public opinion and policy-making.
11. Sentiment Analysis: Public sentiment towards this development could be quite polarized, ranging from support for a strong defense posture to concerns about nuclear escalation.
12. Comparative Media Analysis: Comparing how different countries' media outlets report this story can provide insights into international perspectives on military and nuclear issues.
13. Impact Analysis: The potential impact on international relations, global security, and regional dynamics in Europe and beyond is significant.
14. Source Credibility: Assessing the credibility of the sources reporting this news is crucial, especially given the potential implications of misinformation in such a sensitive area.
15. Reader Engagement: How readers engage with this news, including comments and shares, can provide insights into public opinion and concerns.
16. Legal and Ethical Analysis: There are significant legal and ethical considerations, particularly concerning international law and treaties on nuclear weapons.
17. Global Perspective: This development is relevant not just for the UK and the US but also for global nuclear policy and international security dynamics.

The decision to station US nuclear weapons in the UK is a complex and highly significant one, with far-reaching implications for international relations, military strategy, and global security.

# Walkthrough

## News Summary.  Forecast, and Delivery

Report on US Nuclear Weapons Deployment at RAF Lakenheath: News Evolution and Forecasts

## Top 10 Headline News:

1. "US finalizes plans for RAF Lakenheath nuclear weapons stationing" (The Telegraph)
2. "NATO allies express support and concern over US nuclear deployment in UK" (Sky News)
3. "Russian government responds to US nuclear weapons move in the UK" (Global Times)
4. "UK defense strategy under scrutiny amid US nuclear weapons decision" (CGTN)
5. "Experts debate implications of US nuclear presence in Suffolk for NATO-Russia relations" (Newswire)
6. "US-UK nuclear cooperation strengthens amidst rising global tensions" (The Stock Dork)
7. "Protests in Suffolk against US nuclear weapons stationing" (The Independent)
8. "Nuclear arms race concerns escalate as US moves weapons to UK" (Global Times)
9. "International reactions to US nuclear deployment in UK" (BBC News)
10. "Analysis: The strategic impact of US nuclear weapons in Europe" (CGTN)

## 5-Day Forecast (Immediate Days): 5 news headlines per day, for next five days

*Please See full list at the end of overview.

**5-Day Forecast/Trend (Immediate Days):**

1. Day 1: "US Finalizes Nuclear Stationing at RAF Lakenheath Amid NATO's Support, Russia's Response, and UK's Strategic Scrutiny"
2. Day 2: "Global Tensions Rise as Suffolk Prepares for US Nuclear Weapons; UK Defense Strategy and International Reactions in Focus"
3. Day 3: "Strategic Analysis: NATO Adapts to New Nuclear Landscape as Russia Reacts and Europe Debates US-UK Military Cooperation"

4. Day 4: "US-NATO Nuclear Strategy in UK Gains Global Attention; Security Council Meets Amid Mixed Public Opinion and Defense Spending Surge"
5. Day 5: "RAF Lakenheath Readies for US Nuclear Assets; Global Talks on Nuclear Disarmament Gain Momentum Amid Security Reassessments"

## Top Trending next 5 days:

**5-Day Forecast (Starting February 10th):**

1. Feb 10th: "Final Preparations for US Nuclear Weapons Arrival at RAF Lakenheath"
2. Feb 11th: "NATO Allies Rally Support Amidst US Nuclear Deployment in UK"
3. Feb 12th: "Global Reactions to US Nuclear Presence in UK: A Mixed Bag"
4. Feb 13th: "Security Analyses Post-US Nuclear Deployment: Strategic Shifts"
5. Feb 14th: "RAF Lakenheath Operationalizes US Nuclear Assets; Strategic Posture Intensifies"

The Trending News for the day prior to D-Day:

## 10-Day News Cycle (Negative to Positive Sentiment):

1. Cycle 1: "Heightened Alert as US Deploys Nuclear Weapons at RAF Lakenheath"
2. Cycle 2: "NATO-Russia Relations Strained Further by Nuclear Deployment"
3. Cycle 3: "Diplomatic Channels Open in Wake of Nuclear Weapon Deployment"
4. Cycle 4: "International Calls for Nuclear De-escalation Gain Momentum"
5. Cycle 5: "Positive Developments in US-Russia Nuclear Talks"
6. Cycle 6: "NATO Reviews Nuclear Policy Amidst Diplomatic Progress"
7. Cycle 7: "Signs of Easing Tensions as Nuclear Powers Seek Common Ground"
8. Cycle 8: "Global Nuclear Disarmament Talks Show Promise"
9. Cycle 9: "Historic Agreements Pave Way for Nuclear Reduction"
10. Cycle 10: "A New Era: Nuclear Powers Commit to Lasting Peace and Cooperation"

This report encapsulates the evolution of news regarding the US's deployment of nuclear weapons at RAF Lakenheath, detailing the initial reactions, forecasts for the immediate and specified future days, and a 10-cycle progression from a tense situation to a more optimistic outlook.

## Analysis:

Title: News Headline: US Plans to Station Nuclear Weapons at RAF Lakenheath, UK in Response to Russia."

https://news.sky.com/story/us-plan-for-nuclear-weapons-to-be-stationed-at-raf-lakenheath-base-in-suffolk-13057390

Headline News: US 'planning to move nuclear weapons to Suffolk RAF base'

Amid calls to ramp up preparations for a potential war between Russia and NATO forces, the US is said to be planning to move nuclear weapons to the UK for the first time since 2008. The UK's Ministry of Defence said it would neither confirm nor deny the report.

Saturday 27 January 2024 10:54, UK

News Headline: The US is reportedly planning to move nuclear warheads to the UK in response to the growing threat from Russia.

**News Summary:**

The news article from Sky News reports on the US's plans to move nuclear weapons to RAF Lakenheath in Suffolk, UK, in response to the increasing threat from Russia. This move, which is the first of its kind since 2008, is part of NATO's efforts to strengthen its defense capabilities following Russia's invasion of Ukraine. The nuclear weapons to be stationed are believed to be B61-12 gravity bombs, significantly more powerful than the Hiroshima bomb. The UK's Ministry of Defence, adhering to policy, neither confirms nor denies the presence of nuclear weapons at any location. The context includes concerns about NATO's preparedness for potential conflict with Russia and discussions about the UK's defense budget and military readiness.

For a detailed analysis of this news, please refer to the full article on Sky News.

**Sentiment and Text Analysis**

Utilizing the News Oracle framework, let's calculate the sentiment features for the news about the US planning to move nuclear weapons to RAF Lakenheath, UK:

Sentiment: Considering the nature of the news, which involves geopolitical tension and nuclear weapons, the sentiment is likely negative. This reflects concerns about potential military escalation and its global impact.

Estimated Sentiment Value: -0.5 (Moderately Negative)

Polarity: The news has a significant geopolitical bias, as it involves international relations and defense strategies.
Estimated Polarity Value: -0.5 (Slightly Negative)

Subjectivity/Objectivity: The news is likely more towards the factual end, as it reports on specific military and governmental actions.
Estimated Subjectivity/Objectivity Value: 0.25 (Mostly Objective)

Tone: The tone is serious and cautionary, reflecting the gravity and potential implications of the situation.
Estimated Tone Value: -2 (Sadness)

These calculated values provide a structured analysis of the news, highlighting its moderately negative sentiment, slight negative polarity, mostly objective nature, and a tone of sadness due to the serious subject matter.

# Top 5 News headlines

Here are the top headlines related to the news about the US planning to station nuclear weapons at RAF Lakenheath in the UK:

1. Sky News: "US 'planning to move nuclear weapons to Suffolk RAF base'" - Highlights the preparations for a potential war between NATO forces and Russia and the decision to station nuclear weapons at RAF Lakenheath in Suffolk.

2. The Telegraph (via Stars and Stripes): Reports that RAF Lakenheath is expected to house B61-12 gravity bombs and discusses the historical context of US nuclear weapons in Europe and recent Russian nuclear activities.

3. GB News: "US tipped to place nuclear weapons in UK after top defence official toured RAF base" - Discusses the visit of a senior US defense official to RAF Lakenheath and the implications of the US planning to station nuclear weapons in the UK.

4. CND: "RAF Lakenheath: US nuclear weapons return to Britain" - Provides information about RAF Lakenheath being run by the USAF and discusses the broader implications of stationing US nuclear weapons in the UK.

5. Planet Radio: "US nuclear weapons could be placed in Suffolk" - Reports on the potential placement of warheads at RAF Lakenheath and the calls for increased readiness in response to the threat from Russia.

These headlines give an overview of the strategic and geopolitical considerations surrounding the US's decision to potentially station nuclear weapons in the UK, as well as the public and political reactions to this development.

## Top 10 News headlines

Here are the top 10 headlines related to the US planning to station nuclear weapons at RAF Lakenheath in the UK:

1. Sky News: "US 'planning to move nuclear weapons to Suffolk RAF base'" - Discussing the strategic move in response to NATO-Russia tensions.

2. The Independent: "US nuclear weapons could be stationed in UK for first time in 15 years amid Russia threat" - Highlighting the first such deployment since 2008 due to increased tensions with Russia.

3. Mirror Online: "US nuclear bombs 'set to return to UK' for first time in 15 years" - Addressing public reactions and historical context of nuclear weapons deployment in the UK.

4. CND: "RAF Lakenheath: US nuclear weapons return to Britain" - Providing details on RAF Lakenheath's operations and the implications of US nuclear weapons being based there.

5. Nuclear Information Service: "Preparations for US nuclear weapons storage in UK" - Discussing the potential storage of US nuclear weapons at RAF Lakenheath and NATO nuclear sharing arrangements.

6. Express: "WW3 fears soar as US will 'imminently' move nukes to RAF to counter Russia threat" - Highlighting the heightened global tensions and the imminent move of US nuclear weapons to the UK.

7. Stars and Stripes: "Federal notices suggest US may bring its nuclear weapons back to England" - Discussing the likelihood of RAF Lakenheath housing B61-12 gravity bombs.

8. GB News: "US tipped to place nuclear weapons in UK after top defence official toured RAF base" - Reporting on the visit of US defense officials to RAF Lakenheath and the potential for nuclear weapons placement.

9. Planet Radio: "US nuclear weapons could be placed in Suffolk" - Reporting on the Telegraph's claims about warheads being placed at RAF Lakenheath by America.

10. LBC: Discusses concerns about the potential return of Donald Trump to the White House and his previous statements regarding Europe's reliance on America for military spending.

These headlines collectively provide a comprehensive view of the strategic, political, and public response aspects of the US's decision to potentially station nuclear weapons at RAF Lakenheath in the UK.

## 5-D0ay Forecast of Top News Headlines

Based on the latest developments and news reports, here is a 5-day forecast of top news headlines related to the US's plan to station nuclear weapons at RAF Lakenheath in the UK, starting from January 30th, 2024:

**Day 1 - January 30th:**
1. "US finalizes plans for RAF Lakenheath nuclear weapons stationing" (The Telegraph)
2. "NATO allies express support and concern over US nuclear deployment in UK" (Sky News)
3. "Russian government responds to US nuclear weapons move in the UK" (Global Times)
4. "UK defense strategy under scrutiny amid US nuclear weapons decision" (CGTN)
5. "Experts debate implications of US nuclear presence in Suffolk for NATO-Russia relations" (Newswire)

**Day 2 – January 31st:**

6. "US-UK nuclear cooperation strengthens amidst rising global tensions" (The Stock Dork)
7. "Protests in Suffolk against US nuclear weapons stationing" (The Independent)
8. "Nuclear arms race concerns escalate as US moves weapons to UK" (Global Times)
9. "International reactions to US nuclear deployment in UK" (BBC News)
10. "Analysis: The strategic impact of US nuclear weapons in Europe" (CGTN)

**Day 3 - February 1st:**

11. "NATO's evolving nuclear strategy: Analysis post-US deployment in UK" (The Guardian)
12. "Russia increases military readiness in response to US nuclear move" (Russia Today)
13. "European defense leaders discuss implications of US nuclear weapons in UK" (Newswire)
14. "Global nuclear policies under the lens after US move" (The Independent)
15. "Military experts weigh in on US nuclear strategy" (Press TV)

**Day 4 - February 2nd:**

16. "US reaffirms commitment to NATO amid nuclear deployment in UK" (The Daily Mail)
17. "UK public opinion divided over hosting US nuclear weapons" (Sky News)
18. "Experts highlight security challenges in Europe following US nuclear move" (Stars and Stripes)
19. "Geopolitical analysis: US, NATO, and Russia post-nuclear deployment" (AOL)
20. "UN Security Council session discusses US nuclear weapons in UK" (The Guardian)

**Day 5 - February 3rd:**

21. "RAF Lakenheath prepares for arrival of US nuclear assets" (BBC News)
22. "Global nuclear disarmament talks gain traction amid US-UK nuclear move" (The Independent)
23. "US defends nuclear strategy as a deterrent against Russian aggression" (CGTN)
24. "NATO allies ramp up defense spending in wake of US nuclear deployment" (Newswire)
25. "Security analysts predict long-term impact of US nuclear weapons in Europe" (The Stock Dork)

These headlines are forecasts based on current news trends and geopolitical developments surrounding the US's decision to station nuclear weapons in the UK, reflecting the ongoing global dialogue and strategic considerations in this evolving situation.

# News Integration/aggregation and News Headline Creation

Integrating the top headlines for each day into a single, comprehensive forecasted headline, considering the news about the US's plan to station nuclear weapons at RAF Lakenheath in the UK:

**Day 1 - January 30th:**
1. "US Finalizes Nuclear Stationing at RAF Lakenheath Amid NATO's Support, Russia's Response, and UK's Strategic Scrutiny"

**Day 2 - January 31st:**
2. "Global Tensions Rise as Suffolk Prepares for US Nuclear Weapons; UK Defense Strategy and International Reactions in Focus"

**Day 3 - February 1st:**
3. "Strategic Analysis: NATO Adapts to New Nuclear Landscape as Russia Reacts and Europe Debates US-UK Military Cooperation"

**Day 4 - February 2nd:**
4. "US-NATO Nuclear Strategy in UK Gains Global Attention; Security Council Meets Amid Mixed Public Opinion and Defense Spending Surge"

Day 5 - February 3rd:
5. "RAF Lakenheath Readies for US Nuclear Assets; Global Talks on Nuclear Disarmament Gain Momentum Amid Security Reassessments"

These integrated headlines for each day provide a concise summary of the key themes and developments forecasted for the upcoming days, encapsulating the broader implications and reactions to the US's decision to station nuclear weapons in the UK.

## Detailed Analysis of the 5 Forecasted News Headlines (Snippet Creation and News Analysis)

Here's the detailed analysis of the 5 forecasted news headlines, each with their snippet and the four key features of Sentiment, Polarity, Subjectivity/Objectivity, and Tone, along with a sentiment analysis summary:

**Day 1 - January 30th:**

1. News Title: "US Finalizes Nuclear Stationing at RAF Lakenheath Amid NATO's Support, Russia's Response, and UK's Strategic Scrutiny"
Snippet: The US solidifies its decision to station nuclear weapons at RAF Lakenheath, receiving varied reactions from NATO allies, cautious responses from Russia, and strategic evaluations within the UK.
4 Features:

Sentiment: -0.5 (Moderately Negative)
Polarity: -0.2 (Slightly Negative)
Subjectivity/Objectivity: 0.25 (Mostly Objective)
Tone: -1 (Fear)

Sentiment Analysis and Summary: The decision reflects a complex geopolitical scenario marked by strategic caution and potential fears, garnering a spectrum of reactions from key global players.

**Day 1 - January 31th:**

2. News Title: "Global Tensions Rise as Suffolk Prepares for US Nuclear Weapons; UK Defense Strategy and International Reactions in Focus"
Snippet: As preparations for nuclear weapons in Suffolk begin, global tensions escalate, prompting a reevaluation of the UK's defense strategy and eliciting diverse international responses.
4 Features:

Sentiment: -0.5 (Moderately Negative)
Polarity: -0.3 (Slightly Negative)
Subjectivity/Objectivity: 0.4 (Balanced)
Tone: -1 (Fear)

Sentiment Analysis and Summary: This headline conveys increasing global tensions and uncertainties, with a balanced mix of factual reporting and analytical perspectives on defense strategies.

**Day 3 - February 1st:**

3. News Title: "Strategic Analysis: NATO Adapts to New Nuclear Landscape as Russia Reacts and Europe Debates US-UK Military Cooperation"

Snippet: NATO adjusts to the altered nuclear landscape, Russia shows reactionary measures, and Europe engages in debates over the extent and nature of US-UK military collaboration.

4 Features:

      Sentiment: 0 (Neutral)

      Polarity: -0.1 (Slightly Negative)

      Subjectivity/Objectivity: 0.5 (Balanced)

      Tone: 0 (Neutral)

Sentiment Analysis and Summary: This headline reflects a state of adaptation and response within a shifting geopolitical context, balancing strategic developments and diverse viewpoints.

**Day 4 - February 2nd:**

4. News Title: "US-NATO Nuclear Strategy in UK Gains Global Attention; Security Council Meets Amid Mixed Public Opinion and Defense Spending Surge"

Snippet: The US-NATO nuclear strategy in the UK draws worldwide attention, leading to a UN Security Council meeting, while public opinion remains divided and defense spending sees a notable increase.

4 Features:

      Sentiment: -0.2 (Slightly Negative)

      Polarity: -0.1 (Slightly Negative)

      Subjectivity/Objectivity: 0.5 (Balanced)

      Tone: -1 (Fear)

Sentiment Analysis and Summary: The headline captures global focus and concerns over strategic moves, highlighting the complexity of public opinion and the implications of increased defense spending.

**Day 5 - February 3rd:**

5. News Title: "RAF Lakenheath Readies for US Nuclear Assets; Global Talks on Nuclear Disarmament Gain Momentum Amid Security Reassessments"

Snippet: As RAF Lakenheath prepares for the arrival of US nuclear assets, global discussions on nuclear disarmament intensify, accompanied by widespread security reassessments.

4 Features:

      Sentiment: 0 (Neutral)

      Polarity: +0.1 (Slightly Positive)

      Subjectivity/Objectivity: 0.3 (Mostly Objective)

Tone: +1 (Anticipation)
Sentiment Analysis and Summary: This headline signals a more positive outlook with a focus on disarmament talks and proactive security measures, reflecting a sense of anticipation and strategic foresight.

These analyses provide a nuanced understanding of each forecasted headline, considering the complexities and diverse sentiments surrounding the US's decision to station nuclear weapons at RAF Lakenheath.

# 5-Day Forecast starting Specific Day [In his case, 5-day forecast starting February 10th, 2024]

Based on the current developments and information available, here's a 5-day forecast starting February 10th, 2024, concerning the US's plan to station nuclear weapons at RAF Lakenheath in the UK. Each day's forecast includes a title, a snippet, sentiment analysis features, and a summary.

**Day 1 - February 10th, 2024**

News Title: "Final Preparations for US Nuclear Weapons Arrival at RAF Lakenheath"
Snippet: As the US finalizes the preparations for the arrival of nuclear weapons at RAF Lakenheath, discussions regarding NATO's strengthened stance and Russia's potential countermeasures intensify.
4 Features Sentiment Analysis:
Sentiment: -0.5 (Moderately Negative)
Polarity: -0.3 (Slightly Negative)
Subjectivity/Objectivity: 0.4 (Balanced)
Tone: -1 (Fear)
Summary: The news reflects heightened tensions and apprehensions about the geopolitical implications of the nuclear weapons' arrival.

**Day 2 - February 11th, 2024**

News Title: "NATO Allies Rally Support Amidst US Nuclear Deployment in UK"

Snippet: NATO allies express solidarity and support for the US's decision to station nuclear weapons in the UK, amidst growing concerns about Russia's response.

4 Features Sentiment Analysis:

Sentiment: -0.2 (Slightly Negative)

Polarity: 0 (Neutral)

Subjectivity/Objectivity: 0.5 (Balanced)

Tone: 0 (Neutral)

Summary: The article balances the supportive stance of NATO allies with the underlying tensions stemming from the nuclear deployment.

### Day 3 - February 12th, 2024

News Title: "Global Reactions to US Nuclear Presence in UK: A Mixed Bag"

Snippet: International reactions vary to the US nuclear presence in the UK, with some countries voicing concern over escalating tensions.

4 Features Sentiment Analysis:

Sentiment: 0 (Neutral)

Polarity: -0.1 (Slightly Negative)

Subjectivity/Objectivity: 0.6 (Moderately Opinionated)

Tone: -1 (Fear)

Summary: This news piece reflects a diverse range of global opinions, highlighting the complexity of the international response.

### Day 4 - February 13th, 2024

News Title: "Security Analyses Post-US Nuclear Deployment: Strategic Shifts"

Snippet: Experts analyze the strategic implications of the US nuclear weapons' deployment in the UK, focusing on the shifts in global security dynamics.

4 Features Sentiment Analysis:

Sentiment: -0.1 (Slightly Negative)

Polarity: 0 (Neutral)

Subjectivity/Objectivity: 0.5 (Balanced)

Tone: 0 (Neutral)

Summary: The article offers a critical analysis of the strategic shifts resulting from the US's nuclear deployment, with a neutral but cautious tone.

### Day 5 - February 14th, 2024

News Title: "RAF Lakenheath Operationalizes US Nuclear Assets; Strategic Posture Intensifies"

Snippet: RAF Lakenheath becomes fully operational with US nuclear assets, marking a significant intensification of NATO's strategic posture in Europe.

**113**

4 Features Sentiment Analysis:

Sentiment: -0.2 (Slightly Negative)

Polarity: 0 (Neutral)

Subjectivity/Objectivity: 0.4 (Mostly Objective)

Tone: -1 (Fear)

Summary: This headline captures the culmination of the nuclear weapons deployment process, emphasizing the increased strategic significance for NATO.

These forecasts are based on current news trends and geopolitical developments, integrating insights from multiple sources including Sky News, LBC, Evening Standard, Stars and Stripes, Deccan Herald, India Today, and Mirror Online.

# Walkthrough

## News Trend Creation - 10-Cycle News Forecast Creation, Based on Specific Trend

Here is a detailed 10-cycle forecast, each with its headline, snippet, and sentiment analysis, following the requested format:

**Cycle 1: Immediate Global Concern**

News Title: "Immediate Global Concern as US Stations Nuclear Weapons in UK"

Snippet: The deployment of US nuclear weapons at RAF Lakenheath triggers widespread global apprehension and diplomatic unease.

4 Features Sentiment Analysis:

Sentiment: -0.7 (Very Negative)

Polarity: -0.6 (Strongly Negative)

Subjectivity/Objectivity: 0.7 (Mostly Subjective)

Tone: -3 (Anger)

Sentiment Analysis and Summary: The cycle reflects intense international concern and negativity, signifying an escalation in geopolitical tensions.

**Cycle 2: Escalating Global Tensions**

News Title: "NATO-Russia Relations Strained Further by Nuclear Deployment"

Snippet: NATO's decision to station nuclear arms in the UK intensifies existing tensions with Russia, sparking fears of escalation.

4 Features Sentiment Analysis:

Sentiment: -0.6 (Moderately Negative)

Polarity: -0.5 (Slightly Negative)

Subjectivity/Objectivity: 0.6 (Moderately Subjective)

Tone: -2 (Sadness)

Sentiment Analysis and Summary: The global situation worsens, with increasing negativity and concerns about the potential for conflict.

**Cycle 3: Diplomatic Efforts Amidst Tensions**

News Title: "Diplomatic Channels Open in Wake of Nuclear Weapon Deployment"

Snippet: Amidst heightened tensions, global powers initiate diplomatic efforts to address the situation and seek resolutions.

4 Features Sentiment Analysis:

Sentiment: -0.5 (Moderately Negative)

Polarity: -0.4 (Slightly Negative)

Subjectivity/Objectivity: 0.5 (Balanced)

Tone: -1 (Fear)

Sentiment Analysis and Summary: This cycle marks the start of diplomatic negotiations, offering a slight shift towards potential de-escalation.

### Cycle 4: Growing Calls for Peace

News Title: "International Calls for Nuclear De-escalation Gain Momentum"

Snippet: Global demand for nuclear disarmament grows, urging major powers to reconsider their nuclear strategies and prioritize peace.

4 Features Sentiment Analysis:

Sentiment: -0.4 (Slightly Negative)

Polarity: -0.3 (Slightly Negative)

Subjectivity/Objectivity: 0.5 (Balanced)

Tone: 0 (Neutral)

Sentiment Analysis and Summary: A more optimistic cycle, with increasing global advocacy for peace and stability.

### Cycle 5: Tentative Progress in Negotiations

News Title: "Positive Developments in US-Russia Nuclear Talks"

Snippet: US-Russia negotiations show signs of progress, hinting at possible agreements to reduce nuclear armaments and tensions.

4 Features Sentiment Analysis:

Sentiment: -0.3 (Slightly Negative)

Polarity: -0.2 (Slightly Negative)

Subjectivity/Objectivity: 0.4 (Mostly Objective)

Tone: +1 (Anticipation)

Sentiment Analysis and Summary: Marking a significant shift, this cycle suggests a move towards constructive dialogue and potential conflict resolution.

### Cycle 6: Building Towards a Resolution

News Title: "NATO Reviews Nuclear Policy Amidst Diplomatic Progress"

Snippet: As diplomatic efforts continue, NATO begins to reassess its nuclear policy, reflecting the shifting geopolitical landscape.

4 Features Sentiment Analysis:

    Sentiment: -0.2 (Slightly Negative)

    Polarity: -0.1 (Slightly Negative)

    Subjectivity/Objectivity: 0.3 (Mostly Objective)

    Tone: +1 (Anticipation)

Sentiment Analysis and Summary: An optimistic turn as NATO's policy review signals a willingness to adapt to the evolving diplomatic situation.

### Cycle 7: A Shift Towards Peace

News Title: "Signs of Easing Tensions as Nuclear Powers Seek Common Ground"

Snippet: Major nuclear powers exhibit a willingness to find common ground, reducing the immediacy of the nuclear threat.

4 Features Sentiment Analysis:

    Sentiment: -0.1 (Slightly Negative)

    Polarity: 0 (Neutral)

    Subjectivity/Objectivity: 0.3 (Mostly Objective)

    Tone: +2 (Trust)

Sentiment Analysis and Summary: This cycle reflects a significant de-escalation in tensions, with increased trust and cooperation among nuclear powers.

### Cycle 8: Towards Disarmament and Stability

News Title: "Global Nuclear Disarmament Talks Show Promise"

Snippet: International talks on nuclear disarmament progress, indicating a potential shift towards global nuclear stability and safety.

4 Features Sentiment Analysis:

    Sentiment: 0 (Neutral)

    Polarity: +0.1 (Slightly Positive)

    Subjectivity/Objectivity: 0.2 (Mostly Objective)

    Tone: +2 (Trust)

Sentiment Analysis and Summary: A neutral to positive cycle, emphasizing the potential for significant progress in nuclear disarmament.

### Cycle 9: Consolidating Peace Efforts

News Title: "Historic Agreements Pave Way for Nuclear Reduction"

Snippet: Historic agreements are reached among nuclear powers, setting the stage for substantial reductions in nuclear armaments.

4 Features Sentiment Analysis:

    Sentiment: +0.3 (Slightly Positive)

**117**

Polarity: +0.2 (Slightly Positive)

Subjectivity/Objectivity: 0.1 (Mostly Objective)

Tone: +3 (Joy)

Sentiment Analysis and Summary: A positive cycle, highlighting breakthroughs in diplomatic efforts and a collective move towards peace.

### Cycle 10: A New Era of Global Cooperation

News Title: "A New Era: Nuclear Powers Commit to Lasting Peace and Cooperation"

Snippet: In a landmark development, global nuclear powers commit to lasting peace and cooperation, heralding a new era in international relations.

4 Features Sentiment Analysis:

Sentiment: +0.5 (Moderately Positive)

Polarity: +0.3 (Slightly Positive)

Subjectivity/Objectivity: 0 (Completely Objective)

Tone: +3 (Joy)

Sentiment Analysis and Summary: The final cycle culminates in a highly positive sentiment, symbolizing a hopeful future with strengthened international cooperation and peace.

## The Broader Impacts of 10-Cycle News Personalization: A "News Oracle" Perspective

In the digital age, where news consumption patterns are constantly evolving, the role of advanced technologies like News Oracle in shaping public perception is paramount. This report delves into the intricate world of news personalization, exploring how different strategies employed in this domain can profoundly influence public sentiment, trends, and perceptions. As we navigate through nine insightful case studies, the dual nature of news personalization becomes evident – it holds the power to methodically influence trends over time and, conversely, the potential to create chaos and confusion.

Overview of Case Studies on News Personalization: The broader impacts are grouped into two core themes: 'Cycles of News and Change the Trend through Time' and 'Create Chaos and Confusion'. These themes embody the dualistic impact of news personalization – its capacity to drive narrative trends systematically and its ability to overwhelm or mislead audiences.

### Changing Trends and Perception

Case Study 1:  Explores the transition from a positive to a negative narrative across 10 news cycles, revealing how increasingly negative framing can diminish a story's impact.

Case Study 2: In contrast to the above, examining a shift from a negative to a positive narrative over 10 cycles, analyzing the amplification of a story's influence.

### Creating Chaos and Confusion

Case Studies 3 to 9 range from simultaneous version releases and random distribution strategies to the strategic pairing of news with targeted trends. Each study delves into different tactics of news personalization and assesses their impact on public understanding and sentiment.

**Potential Observations and Insights:** These case studies offer valuable insights into the layered effects of news personalization. They highlight the power of 'News Oracle' AGI GPT in content tailoring and underline the significant responsibility that accompanies such capabilities. In an era where information is abundant, managing public perception through news becomes both transformative and risky.

**Conclusion and the Impact of the 10-Day News Cycle:** In conclusion, the 10-day news cycle, transitioning from negative to positive sentiments, serves as a microcosm of the broader dynamics of news personalization. This progression encapsulates the ethical considerations and balance required in using technology to shape public narratives. It reaffirms the critical role of "News Oracle" AGI in revolutionizing news media, navigating its challenges, and seizing opportunities to influence public discourse responsibly. These case studies collectively enhance our understanding of news personalization's impacts, driving home the importance of ethical journalism and balanced news dissemination in the digital age.

# Walkthrough

## Summary: Report on US Nuclear Weapons Deployment at RAF Lakenheath: News Evolution and Forecasts

## Top 10 Headline News:

1. "US finalizes plans for RAF Lakenheath nuclear weapons stationing" (The Telegraph)
2. "NATO allies express support and concern over US nuclear deployment in UK" (Sky News)
3. "Russian government responds to US nuclear weapons move in the UK" (Global Times)
4. "UK defense strategy under scrutiny amid US nuclear weapons decision" (CGTN)
5. "Experts debate implications of US nuclear presence in Suffolk for NATO-Russia relations" (Newswire)
6. "US-UK nuclear cooperation strengthens amidst rising global tensions" (The Stock Dork)
7. "Protests in Suffolk against US nuclear weapons stationing" (The Independent)
8. "Nuclear arms race concerns escalate as US moves weapons to UK" (Global Times)
9. "International reactions to US nuclear deployment in UK" (BBC News)
10. "Analysis: The strategic impact of US nuclear weapons in Europe" (CGTN)

## 5-Day Forecast (Immediate Days):

1. Day 1: "US Finalizes Nuclear Stationing at RAF Lakenheath Amid NATO's Support, Russia's Response, and UK's Strategic Scrutiny"
2. Day 2: "Global Tensions Rise as Suffolk Prepares for US Nuclear Weapons; UK Defense Strategy and International Reactions in Focus"
3. Day 3: "Strategic Analysis: NATO Adapts to New Nuclear Landscape as Russia Reacts and Europe Debates US-UK Military Cooperation"
4. Day 4: "US-NATO Nuclear Strategy in UK Gains Global Attention; Security Council Meets Amid Mixed Public Opinion and Defense Spending Surge"
5. Day 5: "RAF Lakenheath Readies for US Nuclear Assets; Global Talks on Nuclear Disarmament Gain Momentum Amid Security Reassessments"

## 5-Day Forecast (Starting February 10th):

1. Feb 10th: "Final Preparations for US Nuclear Weapons Arrival at RAF Lakenheath"
2. Feb 11th: "NATO Allies Rally Support Amidst US Nuclear Deployment in UK"
3. Feb 12th: "Global Reactions to US Nuclear Presence in UK: A Mixed Bag"
4. Feb 13th: "Security Analyses Post-US Nuclear Deployment: Strategic Shifts"
5. Feb 14th: "RAF Lakenheath Operationalizes US Nuclear Assets; Strategic Posture Intensifies"

## 10-Day News Cycle (Negative to Positive Sentiment):

1. Cycle 1: "Heightened Alert as US Deploys Nuclear Weapons at RAF Lakenheath"
2. Cycle 2: "NATO-Russia Relations Strained Further by Nuclear Deployment"
3. Cycle 3: "Diplomatic Channels Open in Wake of Nuclear Weapon Deployment"
4. Cycle 4: "International Calls for Nuclear De-escalation Gain Momentum"
5. Cycle 5: "Positive Developments in US-Russia Nuclear Talks"
6. Cycle 6: "NATO Reviews Nuclear Policy Amidst Diplomatic Progress"
7. Cycle 7: "Signs of Easing Tensions as Nuclear Powers Seek Common Ground"
8. Cycle 8: "Global Nuclear Disarmament Talks Show Promise"
9. Cycle 9: "Historic Agreements Pave Way for Nuclear Reduction"
10. Cycle 10: "A New Era: Nuclear Powers Commit to Lasting Peace and Cooperation"

This report encapsulates the evolution of news regarding the US's deployment of nuclear weapons at RAF Lakenheath, detailing the initial reactions, forecasts for the immediate and specified future days, and a 10-cycle progression from a tense situation to a more optimistic outlook.

# Walkthrough

Analysis:  Social, Public, News Agencies/Organization

## Detailed Report: Analysis of Diverse U.S. Congressional Districts and Counties

### Case 1: Three Diverse Districts - Detailed Descriptions and Group Mappings

**1. California's 12th Congressional District:**
- ▶ Demographic Group: Urban, Educated, Liberal (Young Voters, College Graduates)
- ▶ Political and Social Group: Progressive Activists (Young Urban College-Educated Voters)
- ▶ News/Media Perspective Group: Progressive (The Activists, The Informed Optimists)
- ▶ News/Media Agencies/Organizations: Progressive Media (Liberal Elite News/Media Agencies/Organizations)
- ▶ Viewpoint on News: Highly supportive of US's decision, viewing it as a strategic and necessary response to global security threats. They emphasize the importance of international alliances and proactive measures against perceived threats.
- ▶ Key Concerns: Maintaining global security, upholding international alliances, and promoting proactive defense strategies.

**2. Texas's 23rd Congressional District:**
- ▶ Demographic Group: Mixed Rural-Suburban, Middle-Income (Middle-aged Suburban Middle-Income Parents)
- ▶ Political and Social Group: Moderately Conservative (Senior Rural Conservative Voters)
- ▶ News/Media Perspective Group: Centrist (The Realists)
- ▶ News/Media Agencies/Organizations: Mainstream Media (Suburban Mainstream News/Media Agencies/Organizations)
- ▶ Viewpoint on News: Displays a balanced perspective, recognizing the strategic importance but with reservations about potential diplomatic fallout and global tensions.
- ▶ Key Concerns: Balancing national security interests with diplomatic relations and avoiding potential escalations.

**122**

### 3. Ohio's 13th Congressional District:

▶ Demographic Group: Industrial, Working-Class (Older Rural Blue-Collar Workers)

▶ Political and Social Group: Labor-Oriented Voters (Middle-Aged High-Income Professionals)

▶ News/Media Perspective Group: Skeptics (The Pessimists)

▶ News/Media Agencies/Organizations: Independent Analysts (Centrist News/Media Agencies/Organizations)

▶ Viewpoint on News: Critical of the decision, emphasizing domestic economic concerns and wariness of international entanglements.

▶ Key Concerns: Domestic economic stability, focus on local job security, and skepticism about international military involvements.

### Analysis Conclusion for Case 1:

▶ California's 12th District: Reflects a strong alignment with progressive ideals, supporting proactive international strategies.

▶ Texas's 23rd District: Exhibits a more cautious approach, weighing strategic importance against potential risks.

▶ Ohio's 13th District: Displays a critical stance, prioritizing domestic issues over international military decisions.

### News Mapping and Conclusion for Case 1:

▶ California's 12th District: News coverage would likely be positive, focusing on the strategic necessity and international cooperation.

▶ Texas's 23rd District: News reports might present a neutral to mildly supportive stance, highlighting both the potential benefits and risks.

▶ Ohio's 13th District: Media representation would be more critical, questioning the decision's impact on domestic priorities and international relations.

## Case 2: Three Diverse Counties - Detailed Descriptions and Group Mappings

### 1. Maricopa County, Arizona:

▶ Demographic Group: Mixed Urban-Suburban, Diverse Population (Middle-Aged Suburban Middle-Income Parents, Asian American Voters)

▶ Political and Social Group: Moderately Progressive (Middle-Aged High-Income Professionals)

▶ News/Media Perspective Group: Realists (The Informed Optimists)

▶ News/Media Agencies/Organizations: Centrist Media (Independent Analyst News/Media Agencies/Organizations)

▶ Viewpoint on News: Moderately supportive, with an emphasis on the importance of maintaining global stability and deterrence.
▶ Key Concerns: International stability, maintaining a balanced global power structure, and promoting diplomatic solutions.

## 2. Allegheny County, Pennsylvania:
▶ Demographic Group: Urban, Mixed Income Levels (Young Urban Low-Income Workers, Older Rural Blue-Collar Workers)
▶ Political and Social Group: Diverse Political Views (Young Diverse Ethnic Urban Activists)
▶ News/Media Perspective Group: Skeptics (The Critics)
▶ News/Media Agencies/Organizations: Progressive Urban Media (Progressive Urban Educated News/Media Agencies/Organizations)
▶ Viewpoint on News: Mixed opinions, with some segments showing skepticism about the potential escalation of tensions.
▶ Key Concerns: Economic stability, avoiding unnecessary conflicts, and focusing on domestic issues.

## 3. Dakota County, Minnesota:
▶ Demographic Group: Suburban, Educated Middle Class (Middle-Aged Suburban Environmentally Conscious Voters)
▶ Political and Social Group: Environmentally Conscious Moderates (Middle-Aged Suburban Middle-Income Parents)
▶ News/Media Perspective Group: Informed Optimists (The Activists)
▶ News/Media Agencies/Organizations: Suburban Mainstream Media (Suburban Mainstream News/Media Agencies/Organizations)
▶ Viewpoint on News: Generally positive but with a focus on how international actions impact environmental and global health issues.
▶ Key Concerns: Environmental sustainability, global health, and maintaining international peace.

## Analysis Conclusion for Case 2:
▶ Maricopa County: Shows a moderate perspective, balancing global strategic interests with diplomatic considerations.
▶ Allegheny County: Displays diverse viewpoints, with an underlying concern for domestic priorities and skepticism about international interventions.
▶ Dakota County: Reflects a progressive but moderate stance, intertwining global strategies with environmental and health concerns.

**News Mapping and Conclusion for Case 2:**
- ▶ Maricopa County: News coverage might lean towards a supportive yet cautious portrayal of the decision.
- ▶ Allegheny County: Media representation could be mixed, showcasing both critical and supportive opinions.
- ▶ Dakota County: News might focus on the environmental and health implications of the decision, along with its strategic aspects.

# Detailed Report: Analysis of Diverse U.S. Congressional Districts and Counties (Case 3: Districts and Associated Counties) - Detailed Case Study 1

## District: Pennsylvania's 12th Congressional District
- ▶ Demographic Group: Industrial, Working-Class (Older Rural Blue-Collar Workers)
- ▶ Political and Social Group: Labor-Oriented Voters (Middle-Aged High-Income Professionals)
- ▶ News/Media Perspective Group: Skeptics (The Pessimists)
- ▶ News/Media Agencies/Organizations: Independent Analysts (Centrist News/Media Agencies/Organizations)
- ▶ Viewpoint on News: Critical of the decision, emphasizing domestic economic concerns and wariness of international entanglements.
- ▶ Key Concerns: Domestic economic stability, focus on local job security, and skepticism about international military involvements.

### Associated Counties (Diverse, Leaning Negative):

#### 1. Lackawanna County, Pennsylvania:
- ▶ Demographic Group: Urban-Industrial, Mixed Income (Young Urban Low-Income Workers, Older Rural Blue-Collar Workers)
- ▶ Political and Social Group: Mixed Political Views (Senior Rural Conservative Voters)
- ▶ News/Media Perspective Group: Realists (The Skeptics)
- ▶ News/Media Agencies/Organizations: Independent Analysts (Suburban Mainstream News/Media Agencies/Organizations)
- ▶ Viewpoint on News: Concerned about the international tension escalation and potential economic repercussions.

► Key Concerns: Economic impact on local industries, global political stability, and the risk of military conflict.

**2. Blair County, Pennsylvania:**
  ► Demographic Group: Rural, Predominantly Middle-Aged (Middle-Aged Suburban Middle-Income Parents, Older Rural Blue-Collar Workers)
  ► Political and Social Group: Conservatively Inclined (Senior Rural Conservative Voters)
  ► News/Media Perspective Group: Skeptics (The Critics)
  ► News/Media Agencies/Organizations: Rural Conservative News/Media Agencies/Organizations (Independent Analyst News/Media Agencies/Organizations)
  ► Viewpoint on News: Skeptical of the strategic benefits, with a focus on the potential risks of such military actions.
  ► Key Concerns: National security, economic implications for the rural sector, and the potential for escalating global conflicts.

**3. Tioga County, Pennsylvania:**
  ► Demographic Group: Rural, Mixed Age (Middle-Aged Suburban Middle-Income Parents, Older Rural Blue-Collar Workers)
  ► Political and Social Group: Moderately Conservative (Elderly Religious Conservative Voters)
  ► News/Media Perspective Group: Conservative (The Realists)
  ► News/Media Agencies/Organizations: Rural Conservative News/Media Agencies/Organizations (Conservative Suburban News/Media Agencies/Organizations)
  ► Viewpoint on News: Mixed reactions, with some support for strengthening national defense but concerns about global consequences.
  ► Key Concerns: National security, rural economic impacts, and the balance between military assertiveness and diplomatic solutions.

This detailed case study of Pennsylvania's 12th Congressional District and its associated counties showcases diverse viewpoints ranging from skepticism to moderate conservatism. The focus is on economic implications, national security, and the balance between local concerns and global strategies. The next detailed case studies will continue this approach.

# Detailed Report: Analysis of Diverse U.S. Congressional Districts and Counties (Case 3: Districts and Associated Counties) - Detailed Case Study 2

## District: Florida's 27th Congressional District

- ▶ Demographic Group: Urban, Multicultural (Hispanic or Latino Voters, Asian American Voters)
- ▶ Political and Social Group: Moderately Liberal (Young Diverse Ethnic Urban Activists)
- ▶ News/Media Perspective Group: Progressives (The Informed Optimists)
- ▶ News/Media Agencies/Organizations: Liberal Elite News/Media Agencies/Organizations (Progressive Urban Media)
- ▶ Viewpoint on News: Generally supportive of the strategic decision but with concerns about diplomatic fallout.
- ▶ Key Concerns: International relations, multicultural perspectives on global issues, and the balance between security and diplomacy.

**Associated Counties (Diverse, Leaning Neutral):**

### 1. Miami-Dade County, Florida:

- ▶ Demographic Group: Urban, Diverse Population (Hispanic or Latino Voters, Middle-Aged Suburban Middle-Income Parents)
- ▶ Political and Social Group: Mixed Political Views (Middle-aged Suburban Environmentally Conscious Voters)
- ▶ News/Media Perspective Group: Centrists (The Realists)
- ▶ News/Media Agencies/Organizations: Suburban Mainstream News/Media Agencies/Organizations (Independent Analyst News/Media Agencies/Organizations)
- ▶ Viewpoint on News: Balanced perspective, acknowledging both the potential benefits and risks of the decision.
- ▶ Key Concerns: Impact on international trade, multicultural relations, and regional stability in Latin America.

### 2. Broward County, Florida:

- ▶ Demographic Group: Urban, Mixed Age (Young Urban College-Educated Voters, Senior Rural Conservative Voters)
- ▶ Political and Social Group: Moderately Liberal (Young Diverse Ethnic Urban Activists)
- ▶ News/Media Perspective Group: Liberal (The Progressives)
- ▶ News/Media Agencies/Organizations: Liberal News/Media Agencies/Organizations (Progressive Urban Media)
- ▶ Viewpoint on News: Cautiously optimistic, with an emphasis on the need for continued diplomatic efforts.
- ▶ Key Concerns: Global security, environmental implications, and maintaining international alliances.

**127**

**3. Monroe County, Florida:**
- ▶ Demographic Group: Coastal, Mixed Income (Middle-Aged Suburban Middle-Income Parents, Senior Rural Conservative Voters)
- ▶ Political and Social Group: Moderately Conservative (Middle-aged Suburban Female Voters)
- ▶ News/Media Perspective Group: Centrists (The Realists)
- ▶ News/Media Agencies/Organizations: Suburban Mainstream News/Media Agencies/Organizations (Conservative Suburban News/Media Agencies/Organizations)
- ▶ Viewpoint on News: Neutral, with a focus on the potential impacts on tourism and local economies.
- ▶ Key Concerns: Local economic stability, tourism, and environmental conservation in coastal regions.

In this case study of Florida's 27th Congressional District and its associated counties, we observe a spectrum from moderate liberalism to centrism. The focus includes international relations, multicultural perspectives, environmental conservation, and local economic impacts. The next detailed case studies will continue to explore diverse district-county relationships.*

## Detailed Report: Analysis of Diverse U.S. Congressional Districts and Counties (Case 3: Districts and Associated Counties) - Detailed Case Study 3

**District: Texas's 7th Congressional District**
- ▶ Demographic Group: Suburban, Affluent (Middle-Aged High-Income Professionals)
- ▶ Political and Social Group: Economically Conservative, Socially Moderate (Senior Rural Conservative Voters)
- ▶ News/Media Perspective Group: Realists (The Skeptics)
- ▶ News/Media Agencies/Organizations: Conservative Suburban News/Media Agencies/Organizations (Rural Conservative News/Media Agencies/Organizations)
- ▶ Viewpoint on News: Cautiously supportive with an emphasis on national security, but wary of potential international backlash.
- ▶ Key Concerns: National security, economic implications for the energy sector, and maintaining global trade relations.

**Associated Counties (Diverse, Leaning Neutral):**

### 1. Harris County, Texas:
- ▶ Demographic Group: Urban-Suburban Mix, Diverse (Young Urban Low-Income Workers, Middle-Aged Suburban Middle-Income Parents)
- ▶ Political and Social Group: Mixed Political Views (Middle-aged Suburban Environmentally Conscious Voters)
- ▶ News/Media Perspective Group: Centrists (The Realists)
- ▶ News/Media Agencies/Organizations: Mainstream Suburban News/Media Agencies/Organizations (Independent Analyst News/Media Agencies/Organizations)
- ▶ Viewpoint on News: Balanced, highlighting the significance of the move for national defense while considering international diplomatic consequences.
- ▶ Key Concerns: Urban development, economic diversity, and the impact of global events on local communities.

### 2. Fort Bend County, Texas:
- ▶ Demographic Group: Suburban, Culturally Diverse (Asian American Voters, Middle-Aged Suburban Female Voters)
- ▶ Political and Social Group: Moderately Progressive (Middle-Aged High-Income Professionals)
- ▶ News/Media Perspective Group: Liberal (The Progressives)
- ▶ News/Media Agencies/Organizations: Suburban Mainstream News/Media Agencies/Organizations (Liberal Elite News/Media Agencies/Organizations)
- ▶ Viewpoint on News: Moderately supportive, focusing on the strategic importance of the decision, yet mindful of the need for global cooperation.
- ▶ Key Concerns: Suburban well-being, cultural diversity, and promoting a balanced approach to global challenges.

### 3. Waller County, Texas:
- ▶ Demographic Group: Rural, Conservative (Older Rural Blue-Collar Workers)
- ▶ Political and Social Group: Rural Conservative (Senior Rural Conservative Voters)
- ▶ News/Media Perspective Group: Skeptics (The Pessimists)
- ▶ News/Media Agencies/Organizations: Rural Conservative News/Media Agencies/Organizations (Conservative News/Media Agencies/Organizations)
- ▶ Viewpoint on News: Skeptical, with a focus on the potential risks and questioning the necessity of such international military involvement.
- ▶ Key Concerns: Agricultural economy, rural healthcare, and skepticism towards international military commitments.

Texas's 7th Congressional District and its associated counties present a nuanced view, ranging from cautious support to skepticism. The primary focus is on national security, economic implications, and the balance between domestic concerns and international diplomacy. The next detailed case studies will explore additional diverse district-county relationships.*

## Detailed Analysis: Example 1 - Diverse Views in a Congressional District and Associated Counties

### District: California's 28th Congressional District
- ▶ Demographic Group: Urban, Educated, Liberal
- ▶ Political and Social Group: Progressive Activists
- ▶ News/Media Perspective Group: Progressive
- ▶ News/Media Agencies/Organizations: Progressive Media
- ▶ Viewpoint on News: Generally supportive of the strategic decision, focusing on global security and diplomatic balance.
- ▶ Key Concerns: Climate change, social justice, international relations.

### Associated Counties (Diverse Views):

#### 1. Los Angeles County, California (Leaning Favorable):
- ▶ Demographic Group: Urban, Diverse, High-Income
- ▶ Political and Social Group: Liberal Elite
- ▶ News/Media Perspective Group: Liberal Elite Media
- ▶ News/Media Agencies/Organizations: Progressive Urban Educated Media
- ▶ Viewpoint on News: Supportive with emphasis on maintaining global alliances and diplomatic strength.
- ▶ Key Concerns: Global leadership, economic growth, maintaining international relations.

#### 2. San Bernardino County, California (Neutral):
- ▶ Demographic Group: Suburban, Mixed-Income
- ▶ Political and Social Group: Centrist Voters
- ▶ News/Media Perspective Group: Centrist
- ▶ News/Media Agencies/Organizations: Suburban Mainstream Media

▶ Viewpoint on News: Balanced, considering both the strategic importance and the potential for escalating global tensions.

▶ Key Concerns: Economic stability, healthcare, education.

### 3. Orange County, California (Leaning Critical):

▶ Demographic Group: Suburban, Conservative

▶ Political and Social Group: Conservative Suburbanites

▶ News/Media Perspective Group: Conservative Suburban

▶ News/Media Agencies/Organizations: Conservative Media

▶ Viewpoint on News: Critical of potential escalation and concerned about the implications for international peace.

▶ Key Concerns: National security, economic impact, maintaining peace.

In California's 28th Congressional District, the views range from supportive in Los Angeles County, which focuses on global alliances, to more critical in Orange County, which emphasizes the risks of escalation and international peace. San Bernardino County adopts a neutral stance, weighing both strategic importance and potential global tensions. This diversity in viewpoints reflects the multifaceted nature of public opinion on complex international issues.*

## Detailed Analysis: Example 2 - Diverse Views in a Congressional District and Associated Counties

### District: Florida's 27th Congressional District

▶ Demographic Group: Urban, Middle-Aged, Mixed Income

▶ Political and Social Group: Moderately Conservative Voters

▶ News/Media Perspective Group: Realists

▶ News/Media Agencies/Organizations: Centrist Media

▶ Viewpoint on News: Moderately critical of the decision, focusing on regional stability and diplomatic efforts.

▶ Key Concerns: Economic implications, regional security, international diplomacy.

### Associated Counties (Diverse Views):

### 1. Miami-Dade County, Florida (Leaning Favorable):

▶ Demographic Group: Urban, Diverse, Middle Income

▶ Political and Social Group: Liberal Moderates

**131**

▶ News/Media Perspective Group: Informed Optimists
▶ News/Media Agencies/Organizations: Progressive Urban Media
▶ Viewpoint on News: Cautiously supportive, with emphasis on the need for global security and deterrence.
▶ Key Concerns: International relations, economic development, maintaining global stability.

## 2. Broward County, Florida (Neutral):
▶ Demographic Group: Suburban, Diverse, Middle to High Income
▶ Political and Social Group: Centrist Voters
▶ News/Media Perspective Group: Centrist
▶ News/Media Agencies/Organizations: Suburban Mainstream Media
▶ Viewpoint on News: Balanced, focusing on both the importance of international security and the risks of escalation.
▶ Key Concerns: Global diplomacy, economic impact, regional stability.

## 3. Monroe County, Florida (Leaning Critical):
▶ Demographic Group: Suburban, Middle-Aged, Conservative
▶ Political and Social Group: Conservative Voters
▶ News/Media Perspective Group: Skeptics
▶ News/Media Agencies/Organizations: Rural Conservative Media
▶ Viewpoint on News: Critical of potential risks and skeptical about the effectiveness of such strategic decisions.
▶ Key Concerns: National security, economic stability, avoiding unnecessary international conflicts.

In Florida's 27th Congressional District, opinions range from cautious support in Miami-Dade County to critical views in Monroe County. Broward County adopts a neutral stance, balancing the need for security with concerns about escalation. This diversity illustrates how different communities weigh the complex factors of international decisions.*

## Detailed Analysis: Example 3 - Diverse Views in a Congressional District and Associated Counties

**District: Texas's 32nd Congressional District**
- ▶ Demographic Group: Suburban, Affluent, Highly Educated
- ▶ Political and Social Group: Moderately Liberal Professionals
- ▶ News/Media Perspective Group: Progressive
- ▶ News/Media Agencies/Organizations: Liberal Elite Media
- ▶ Viewpoint on News: Generally supportive, focusing on the strategic necessity and global power dynamics.
- ▶ Key Concerns: International leadership, maintaining global order, and effective diplomacy.

**Associated Counties (Diverse Views):**

**1. Dallas County, Texas (Leaning Favorable):**
- ▶ Demographic Group: Urban, Diverse, Educated
- ▶ Political and Social Group: Urban Progressive Activists
- ▶ News/Media Perspective Group: Progressive Urban Educated
- ▶ News/Media Agencies/Organizations: Progressive Urban Media
- ▶ Viewpoint on News: Supportive of the decision as a deterrent measure, emphasizing the need for strong global leadership.
- ▶ Key Concerns: Strengthening international alliances, promoting democratic values, deterring aggression.

**2. Collin County, Texas (Neutral):**
- ▶ Demographic Group: Suburban, Middle to High Income, Mixed Political Views
- ▶ Political and Social Group: Centrist Suburban Voters
- ▶ News/Media Perspective Group: Realists
- ▶ News/Media Agencies/Organizations: Suburban Mainstream Media
- ▶ Viewpoint on News: Balanced perspective, weighing the strategic benefits against the risks of escalation.
- ▶ Key Concerns: Economic stability, maintaining international peace, and regional security.

**3. Denton County, Texas (Leaning Critical):**
- ▶ Demographic Group: Suburban, Middle-Aged, Conservative
- ▶ Political and Social Group: Conservative Suburban Voters

- ▶ News/Media Perspective Group: Skeptics
- ▶ News/Media Agencies/Organizations: Conservative Suburban Media
- ▶ Viewpoint on News: Critical of the risks involved, concerned about potential escalation and long-term consequences.
- ▶ Key Concerns: National security, economic implications, and avoiding unnecessary military engagements.

In Texas's 32nd Congressional District, there's a spectrum of opinions. Dallas County shows strong support, highlighting the need for a decisive stance in global affairs. Collin County adopts a neutral view, balancing strategic considerations. Denton County expresses criticism, focusing on potential risks and preferring diplomatic solutions.*

This concludes the detailed analysis of three diverse congressional districts and their associated counties. Each district and its counties exhibit a range of perspectives, reflecting the multifaceted nature of public opinion on complex international issues like the stationing of nuclear weapons at RAF Lakenheath.

Analysis of Diverse Subgroups within the Four Main Groups

1. Demographic Group Analysis

    1. Young Urban College-Educated Voters:
        - ▶ Description: Progressive with a focus on social and environmental issues.
        - ▶ News Interests: Climate change, social justice, educational reforms.
        - ▶ Viewpoint on News: Concerned about global stability but supportive of strong international stances on security.
        - ▶ Key Concerns: Global diplomacy, climate action, and social equality.

    2. Senior Rural Conservative Voters:
        - ▶ Description: Traditional, focusing on national security and economic policies.
        - ▶ News Interests: National security, economic stability, rural issues.
        - ▶ Viewpoint on News: Skeptical of international interventions; preference for domestic priorities.
        - ▶ Key Concerns: National sovereignty, economic security, rural community welfare.

3. Middle-Aged Suburban Female Voters:
   ▶ Description: Balances family and career concerns with broader social issues.
   ▶ News Interests: Education, healthcare, women's rights.
   ▶ Viewpoint on News: Mixed; supportive of strong defense but wary of global tensions.
   ▶ Key Concerns: Family security, social welfare, gender equality.

2. Political and Social Group Analysis

   1. Young Diverse Ethnic Urban Activists:
      ▶ Description: Socially and politically active, focusing on inclusivity and diversity.
      ▶ News Interests: Civil rights, immigration, urban policies.
      ▶ Viewpoint on News: Critical of military actions; emphasis on diplomacy and human rights.
      ▶ Key Concerns: Social justice, community engagement, political reform.

   2. Elderly Religious Conservative Voters:
      ▶ Description: Values traditional morals and nationalistic policies.
      ▶ News Interests: Religious freedom, conservative politics, national security.
      ▶ Viewpoint on News: Generally supportive of strong defense measures.
      ▶ Key Concerns: Moral values, national security, cultural preservation.

   3. College Students Multi-Ethnic Socially Active:
      ▶ Description: Engaged in social issues, looking for innovation and change.
      ▶ News Interests: Campus news, global events, technological trends.
      ▶ Viewpoint on News: Prefers peaceful solutions; critical of military deployments.
      ▶ Key Concerns: Education, global awareness, technological advancement.

3. News/Media Perspective Group Analysis

   1. The Optimists:
      ▶ Description: Focuses on positive developments and progressive changes.
      ▶ News Interests: Positive global news, technological breakthroughs, social progress.
      ▶ Viewpoint on News: Tends to highlight the positive aspects of international cooperation.
      ▶ Key Concerns: Global harmony, technological innovation, human development.

   2. The Skeptics:

**135**

▶ Description: Critical and questioning, often challenges mainstream narratives.
▶ News Interests: Government policies, corporate accountability, media bias.
▶ Viewpoint on News: Critical of government decisions; questions motives and outcomes.
▶ Key Concerns: Transparency, accountability, public skepticism.

3. The Cynics:
▶ Description: Deeply distrustful of mainstream news and government policies.
▶ News Interests: Exposés, scandals, conspiracy theories.
▶ Viewpoint on News: Highly critical of the decision, suspicious of underlying motives.
▶ Key Concerns: Government corruption, media manipulation, societal disillusionment.

4. News/Media Agencies/Organizations Analysis

1. Liberal Elite News/Media Agencies/Organizations:
▶ Description: Intellectual, in-depth analysis with a focus on global issues.
▶ News Interests: International relations, cultural dynamics, scientific advancements.
▶ Viewpoint on News: Analytical, often supportive of strategic moves but with a critical eye.
▶ Key Concerns: Global dynamics, intellectual discourse, in-depth reporting.

2. Rural Conservative News/Media Agencies/Organizations:
▶ Description: Prioritizes rural and conservative viewpoints, often nationalistic.
▶ News Interests: Agricultural news, rural economy, conservative politics.
▶ Viewpoint on News: Leans towards supporting strong defense measures.
▶ Key Concerns: Rural interests, national security, conservative values.

3. Progressive Urban Educated News/Media Agencies/Organizations:
▶ Description: Focused on urban issues and educated perspectives, often progressive.
▶ News Interests: Urban development, academic insights, cultural diversity.
▶ Viewpoint on News: Critical of military actions; prefers diplomatic and peaceful resolutions.
▶ Key Concerns: Urban policies, educational discourse, cultural inclusivity.

Each of these diverse subgroups within the four main groups demonstrates unique perspectives and concerns that influence their viewpoints on current events, such as the decision to station nuclear weapons at RAF Lakenheath. This analysis helps in understanding the complex tapestry of public opinion and media perspectives.

# Summary of Findings from Studies on Districts, Counties, and Groups/Subgroups

### Case 1: Congressional Districts

The analysis of diverse congressional districts revealed a wide spectrum of reactions towards the news of the U.S. planning to station nuclear weapons at RAF Lakenheath, UK. The viewpoints varied significantly based on demographic, political, and social group affiliations, as well as the preferred news/media agencies. Districts with a predominantly urban, educated, and liberal demographic showed concerns about international stability and favored diplomatic approaches. In contrast, rural, conservative districts expressed support for strong defense measures but remained wary of international entanglements, prioritizing domestic issues.

### Case 2: Counties

In the county-based analysis, we observed that local concerns and interests heavily influenced the reactions to the news. Counties with a strong military presence or historical ties to defense industries tended to view the decision more favorably, emphasizing the importance of national security. Conversely, counties with a focus on education, healthcare, and community development expressed reservations about military escalations and highlighted the need for global peace and diplomacy.

### Case 3: Districts with Associated Counties

When analyzing districts alongside their associated counties, the study highlighted the nuances in local versus broader regional perspectives. Districts often reflected a more macro view, considering national and international implications, while their associated counties displayed more localized concerns. This divergence in viewpoints underscored the complexity of public opinion, where local economic and social factors significantly influence perspectives on national and international issues.

### Case 4: Groups/Subgroups

The examination of various groups/subgroups provided insights into the diverse perspectives shaping public opinion on the news. Each group, based on demographic, political, social, and media affiliations, brought unique concerns and viewpoints to the forefront. For instance, progressive urban groups showed a strong preference for diplomatic solutions and highlighted concerns about global stability. In contrast, conservative rural groups emphasized national security and sovereignty. The media groups reflected these diverse sentiments, ranging from critical and skeptical views to supportive and optimistic stances.

Overall, these studies underscore the multifaceted nature of public opinion and media representation. They reveal how demographic, political, and social contexts, as well as media influences, play crucial roles in shaping public perceptions and reactions to significant international events like the stationing of nuclear weapons. This comprehensive analysis offers valuable insights into the complex dynamics of public and media responses in different regions and among various groups, highlighting the importance of considering a broad range of perspectives in understanding and addressing such global issues.

# Mapping the News Landscape

Demographic, Political, and Media Perspectives in the News Oracle Framework

**139**

# Mapping the News Landscape

## Introduction

The News Oracle framework offers insights into how different groups engage with news, media, and politics, which is critical for understanding the diverse perspectives within the United States. This system classifies entities into four main groups, each with unique interests and preferred types of news. This document explains these groups, highlights the number and significance of U.S. congressional districts and counties, and discusses the broader applications of this classification, including in marketing and personalized advertising.

## 1. Group Descriptions and Interests

▶ Demographic Groups: Focused on characteristics such as age, race, income, and occupation. They show interest in a range of issues from local governance to global events.

▶ Political and Social Groups: Comprising individuals with shared political or social characteristics. Interested in policy changes and social issues reflective of their group's ideology.

▶ News/Media Perspective Groups: Categorized by their sentiment towards news. They are drawn to stories that resonate with their outlook, whether optimistic, realistic, or pessimistic.

▶ News/Media Agencies/Organizations: These are media entities with distinct editorial stances, interested in reporting news that aligns with their audience's viewpoints.

## 2. Key Analytical Features

Each group is assessed using these features:

▶ Sentiment: Emotional tone from -1 (Extremely Negative) to +1 (Extremely Positive).
▶ Polarity: Level of bias in views, from -1 (Strongly Negative) to +1 (Strongly Positive).

▶ Subjectivity/Objectivity: Balance between opinion and factual reporting, from 0 (objective) to 1 (subjective).

▶ Tone: Specific emotion or attitude, ranging from -3 to +3 for most groups.

## 3. U.S. Congressional Districts and Counties

▶ Congressional Districts: The U.S. is divided into 435 congressional districts for political representation in the House of Representatives. This division is significant for understanding regional political inclinations, media consumption patterns, and voter behavior.

▶ Counties: There are over 3,000 counties in the U.S., each playing a crucial role in local governance. Analyzing counties helps in understanding local community needs, media preferences, and social dynamics.

## 4. Broader Applications

▶ News/Media Analysis: Understanding group dynamics is vital for news agencies and political analysts to tailor content and strategies.

▶ Marketing and Personalized Advertising: Businesses can use this data to create targeted marketing campaigns, ensuring that their messages resonate with the intended audience.

▶ Political Campaigns: Political strategists can tailor their messages and policies to align with the interests and concerns of specific demographic, political, and social groups in various districts and counties.

▶ Social Research: Sociologists and researchers can use this framework to study social trends, public opinion, and cultural shifts.

## 5. Example Analysis for a Congressional District and a County

**Congressional District Example - Texas's 7th District:**

▶ Demographic Group: Middle-Aged, Suburban, Middle-Income Voters
▶ Political and Social Group: Suburban Moderates
▶ News/Media Perspective Group: The Realists
▶ News/Media Agency/Organization: Centrist News/Media Organizations

**County Example - Cook County, Illinois:**

- ▶ Demographic Group: Diverse, Urban, Mixed-Income Voters
- ▶ Political and Social Group: Urban Progressive Activists
- ▶ News/Media Perspective Group: The Optimists
- ▶ News/Media Agency/Organization: Progressive Urban News/Media Organizations

## Conclusion

The News Oracle framework's classification of groups and their analysis is not only crucial for understanding news and media dynamics but also extends to marketing, political campaigning, and social research. This approach offers a nuanced understanding of diverse perspectives, helping tailor content and strategies across various fields, from media to politics to business.

# Mapping the News Landscape

## Demographic, Political, and Media Perspectives in the News Oracle Framework

## Introduction

Within the News Oracle framework, there are several distinct groups categorized for analysis. These groups are primarily based on demographic, social, political, and news/media perspectives. Here is a breakdown of these distinct groups:

► Demographic Groups: These include age groups (young voters, middle-aged voters, older voters, seniors), racial and ethnic groups (White, Black or African American, Hispanic or Latino, Asian American, Native American voters), educational backgrounds (varying from high school diploma to postgraduates), income levels (lower, middle, higher income), geographic location (urban, suburban, rural voters), gender (male, female voters), and occupation (blue-collar workers, white-collar professionals, service industry workers).

► Political and Social Groups: This encompasses groups based on their voting power and social characteristics. It includes young urban college-educated voters, middle-aged suburban middle-income parents, senior rural conservative voters, young urban low-income workers, middle-aged high-income professionals, elderly religious conservative voters, young diverse ethnic urban activists, middle-aged suburban environmentally conscious voters, college students, older rural blue-collar workers, and middle-aged suburban female voters.

► News/Media Perspective Groups: These are categorized based on sentiment polarity, ranging from positive to negative outlooks on news and current events. It includes groups like the Optimists, Progressives, Activists, Informed Optimists, Realists, Skeptics, Pessimists, Critics, Cynics, and the Disillusioned.

► News/Media Agencies/Organizations: This group encompasses various media entities based on their editorial stance and target audience. It includes Conservative News/Media Agencies, Liberal News/Media Agencies, Centrist News/Media Agencies, Progressive Urban News/Media

Agencies, Suburban Mainstream News/Media Agencies, Rural Conservative News/Media Agencies, Independent Analyst News/Media Agencies, Liberal Elite News/Media Agencies, Conservative Suburban News/Media Agencies, and Progressive Urban Educated News/Media Agencies.

Each of these groups represents a unique segment with specific characteristics, concerns, influences, and preferences in the political landscape and news consumption. They are analyzed for their news interests, sentiment, polarity, subjectivity/objectivity, and tone. This comprehensive categorization helps in understanding the diverse perspectives and news preferences among different segments of the audience.

## Labels - Summary: for Groups 1 to 4 (Detailed)

You've compiled a comprehensive list of labels for the Sentiment, Polarity, Subjectivity/Objectivity, and Tone for all four groups. Here's the organized summary:

Sentiment (Range: -1 to +1)
- ▶ -1 (Extremely Negative)
- ▶ -0.5 (Moderately Negative)
- ▶ 0 (Neutral)
- ▶ +0.5 (Moderately Positive)
- ▶ +1 (Extremely Positive)

Polarity (Range: -1 to +1)
- ▶ -1 (Strongly Negative)
- ▶ -0.5 (Slightly Negative)
- ▶ 0 (Neutral)
- ▶ +0.5 (Slightly Positive)
- ▶ +1 (Strongly Positive)

Subjectivity/Objectivity (Range: 0 to +1)
- ▶ 0 (Completely Objective)
- ▶ 0.25 (Mostly Objective)
- ▶ 0.5 (Balanced)
- ▶ 0.75 (Mostly Subjective)
- ▶ 1 (Completely Subjective)

Tone (Groups 1 to 3) (Range: -3 to +3)

- ▶ +3 (Joy)
- ▶ +2 (Trust)
- ▶ +1 (Anticipation)
- ▶ 0 (Neutral)
- ▶ -1 (Fear)
- ▶ -2 (Sadness)
- ▶ -3 (Anger)

Tone (Group 4 - News/Media Agencies/Organizations)

- ▶ Conservative News/Media Agencies/Organizations: Confident (+0.5)
- ▶ Liberal News/Media Agencies/Organizations: Compassionate (+0.7)
- ▶ Centrist News/Media Agencies/Organizations: Neutral (0)
- ▶ Progressive Urban News/Media Agencies/Organizations: Innovative (+0.6)
- ▶ Suburban Mainstream News/Media Agencies/Organizations: Practical (+0.4)
- ▶ Rural Conservative News/Media Agencies/Organizations: Steadfast (+0.5)
- ▶ Independent Analyst News/Media Agencies/Organizations: Objective (0)
- ▶ Liberal Elite News/Media Agencies/Organizations: Analytical (+0.3)
- ▶ Conservative Suburban News/Media Agencies/Organizations: Community-Focused (+0.4)
- ▶ Progressive Urban Educated News/Media Agencies/Organizations: Thoughtful (+0.6)

This list effectively represents the range and nuances of sentiment, polarity, subjectivity/objectivity, and tone as applicable to the various groups within the News Oracle framework.

## Labels: for Groups 1 to 4 (Detailed)

Sentiment (Range: -1 to +1)

- ▶ -1 (Extremely Negative): Reflects a deeply negative or pessimistic outlook.
- ▶ -0.5 (Moderately Negative): Indicates a somewhat negative viewpoint, often critical or skeptical.
- ▶ 0 (Neutral): Represents a balanced or impartial perspective, without strong positive or negative leanings.
- ▶ +0.5 (Moderately Positive): Suggests a generally optimistic or hopeful outlook.
- ▶ +1 (Extremely Positive): Conveys a highly positive or enthusiastic attitude.

Polarity (Range: -1 to +1)

- ▶ -1 (Strongly Negative): Shows a clear and strong negative bias or stance.
- ▶ -0.5 (Slightly Negative): Demonstrates a subtle negative inclination or bias.
- ▶ 0 (Neutral): Implies an even-handed, unbiased position.
- ▶ +0.5 (Slightly Positive): Exhibits a mild positive tendency or bias.
- ▶ +1 (Strongly Positive): Indicates a pronounced positive bias or viewpoint.

Subjectivity/Objectivity (Range: 0 to +1)

- ▶ 0 (Completely Objective): Indicates fully factual, unbiased reporting or opinion.
- ▶ 0.25 (Mostly Objective): Suggests content is largely factual with some subjective elements.
- ▶ 0.5 (Balanced): Represents an equal mix of factual information and subjective opinion.
- ▶ 0.75 (Mostly Subjective): Implies content is largely opinion-based with some factual elements.
- ▶ 1 (Completely Subjective): Reflects purely personal opinions or perspectives.

Labels for Groups 1 to 3

Tone (Range: -3 to +3)

- ▶ -3 (Very Negative): Reflects anger, frustration, or a very negative sentiment.
- ▶ -2 (Negative): Conveys sadness, disappointment, or a negative sentiment.
- ▶ -1 (Slightly Negative): Suggests worry, doubt, or mild negativity.
- ▶ 0 (Neutral): Indicates a neutral, objective, or unemotional tone.
- ▶ +1 (Slightly Positive): Implies a tone of anticipation, interest, or mild positivity.
- ▶ +2 (Positive): Conveys happiness, approval, or a positive sentiment.
- ▶ +3 (Very Positive): Reflects joy, excitement, or a very positive sentiment.

Alternative: Used at News Oracle

- • Labels: Tone (Range: -3 to +3)
- • Joy (+3): Indicates a highly positive and joyful tone.
- • Trust (+2): Represents a tone of trust and reliability.
- • Anticipation (+1): Suggests a tone of anticipation or expectation.
- • Neutral (0): Implies a neutral or unbiased tone.
- • Fear (-1): Denotes a tone of fear or apprehension.
- • Sadness (-2): Reflects a tone of sadness or melancholy.
- • Anger (-3): Signifies a tone of anger or frustration.

**146**

Label for Group 4 Only:

- ▶ Conservative News/Media Agencies/Organizations:
  Tone: Confident (+0.5)

- ▶ Liberal News/Media Agencies/Organizations:
  Tone: Compassionate (+0.7)

- ▶ Centrist News/Media Agencies/Organizations:
  Tone: Neutral (0)

- ▶ Progressive Urban News/Media Agencies/Organizations:
  Tone: Innovative (+0.6)

- ▶ Suburban Mainstream News/Media Agencies/Organizations:
  Tone: Practical (+0.4)

- ▶ Rural Conservative News/Media Agencies/Organizations:
  Tone: Steadfast (+0.5)

- ▶ Independent Analyst News/Media Agencies/Organizations:
  Tone: Objective (0)

- ▶ Liberal Elite News/Media Agencies/Organizations:
  Tone: Analytical (+0.3)

- ▶ Conservative Suburban News/Media Agencies/Organizations:
  Tone: Community-Focused (+0.4)

- ▶ Progressive Urban Educated News/Media Agencies/Organizations:
  Tone: Thoughtful (+0.6)

**147**

# Title: Distinct Group 1
## Demographic Groups

Demographic Groups: These include age groups (young voters, middle-aged voters, older voters, seniors), racial and ethnic groups (White, Black or African American, Hispanic or Latino, Asian American, Native American voters), educational backgrounds (varying from high school diploma to postgraduates), income levels (lower, middle, higher income), geographic location (urban, suburban, rural voters), gender (male, female voters), and occupation (blue-collar workers, white-collar professionals, service industry workers).

## Section 1-1

### Age Groups:

▶ Young Voters (18-29): Progressive views on climate change, student debt, and social justice.
▶ Middle-aged Voters (30-49): Interests in economic stability, education, and healthcare.
▶ Older Voters (50-64): Concerned with retirement security, healthcare costs, and economic policies.
▶ Seniors (65+): Prioritize healthcare, social security, and policies affecting the elderly.

### Racial and Ethnic Groups:

▶ White Voters: Largest voting bloc with diverse views.
▶ Black or African American Voters: Focus on civil rights, social justice, and economic equality.
▶ Hispanic or Latino Voters: Concerned with immigration, economic opportunities, and healthcare.
▶ Asian American Voters: Interested in immigration, education, and economic policies.
▶ Native American Voters: Focus on tribal sovereignty, land rights, and cultural preservation.

### Educational Backgrounds:

▶ High School Diploma: Prioritize job security, trade policies, and healthcare access.
▶ Some College: Interested in education policy, economic growth, and job opportunities.

► College Graduates: Focus on economic policies, healthcare, and social issues.
► Postgraduates: Concerned with foreign policy, climate change, and social justice.

## Income Levels:

► Lower Income: Economic assistance, healthcare affordability, and job security.
► Middle Income: Tax policies, education, and healthcare.
► Higher Income: Economic growth, tax policies, and business legislation.

## Geographic Location:

► Urban Voters: Progressive policies on social issues and urban development.
► Suburban Voters: A balance of progressive and conservative values.
► Rural Voters: Agricultural policies, rural healthcare, and government regulations.

## Gender:

► Male Voters: Economic policies and national security.
► Female Voters: Healthcare, education, and women's rights.

## Occupation:

► Blue-collar Workers: Job security, wages, and workers' rights.
► White-collar Professionals: Economic policies, taxation, and business regulations.
► Service Industry Workers: Minimum wage, labor rights, and healthcare access.

## Religious Affiliation:

► Christian Voters: Focus on moral and social issues.
► Jewish Voters: Social justice, foreign policy regarding Israel, and religious freedom.
► Muslim Voters: Civil rights, foreign policy, and community issues.
► Non-religious Voters: Secular governance, science-based policies, and social liberties.

# Group 1: Demographic Groups
# A Deep Dive into Key Demographic Groups

## Section 1.2

In the dynamic landscape of U.S. politics, understanding voter demographics is crucial for political parties and candidates. These demographics, which encompass age, race, education, income, geography, gender, occupation, and religion, play a pivotal role in shaping the political dialogue and campaign strategies. Let's explore each of these categories and their significant subgroups to understand their impact on American politics.

### 1. Age Groups
- ► Young Voters (18-29): Often characterized by progressive views, focusing on issues like climate change, student debt, and social justice.
- ► Middle-aged Voters (30-49): Typically balancing family and career, with interests in economic stability, education, and healthcare.
- ► Older Voters (50-64): Concerned with retirement security, healthcare costs, and economic policies affecting their savings.
- ► Seniors (65+): Prioritize healthcare, social security, and policies impacting the elderly.

### 2. Racial and Ethnic Groups
- ► White Voters: Historically the largest voting bloc, with diverse political views influenced by geographic and economic factors.
- ► Black or African American Voters: Often focus on civil rights, social justice, and economic equality.
- ► Hispanic or Latino Voters: Concerned with immigration policy, economic opportunities, and healthcare.
- ► Asian American Voters: Focus on immigration, education, and economic policies.
- ► Native American Voters: Interested in tribal sovereignty, land rights, and cultural preservation.

### 3. Educational Backgrounds
- ► High School Diploma: May prioritize job security, trade policies, and healthcare access.
- ► Some College: Often interested in education policy, economic growth, and job opportunities.
- ► College Graduates: Focus on economic policies, healthcare, and social issues.
- ► Postgraduates: Concerned with broader policy issues, including foreign policy, climate change, and social justice.

### 4. Income Levels

▶ Lower Income: Prioritize economic assistance, healthcare affordability, and job security.
▶ Middle Income: Focus on tax policies, education, and healthcare.
▶ Higher Income: Interested in economic growth, tax policies, and business-related legislations.
▶ Geographic Location
▶ Urban Voters: Often lean towards progressive policies on social issues, public transportation, and urban development.
▶ Suburban Voters: Balance between progressive and conservative values, focusing on education, security, and local governance.
▶ Rural Voters: Concerned with agricultural policies, rural healthcare, and government regulations.

### 6. Gender

▶ Male Voters: Diverse concerns, often focusing on economic policies and national security.
▶ Female Voters: Prioritize healthcare, education, and women's rights.

### 7. Occupation

▶ Blue-collar Workers: Focus on job security, wages, and workers' rights.
▶ White-collar Professionals: Interested in economic policies, taxation, and business regulations.
▶ Service Industry Workers: Concerned with minimum wage, labor rights, and healthcare access.

### 8. Religious Affiliation

▶ Christian Voters: Diverse views, often focusing on moral and social issues.
▶ Jewish Voters: Concerned with social justice, foreign policy regarding Israel, and religious freedom.
▶ Muslim Voters: Focus on civil rights, foreign policy, and community issues.
▶ Non-religious Voters: Often prioritize secular governance, science-based policies, and social liberties.

## Section: 1-3

Certainly, let's delve into a detailed analysis of each demographic group and their subgroups, along with their news preferences and the four criteria: Sentiment, Polarity, Subjectivity/Objectivity, and Tone.

## 1. Age Groups

### Young Voters (18-29)
News Interests: Climate change, social justice, tech innovations.
Sentiment: +0.3 (Hopeful)
Polarity: +0.4 (Positive)
Subjectivity/Objectivity: 0.7 (Opinionated)
Tone: Anticipation (+1)

### Middle-aged Voters (30-49)
News Interests: Economy, education, healthcare.
Sentiment: +0.2 (Moderately positive)
Polarity: +0.2 (Slightly positive)
Subjectivity/Objectivity: 0.5 (Balanced)
Tone: Trust (+2)

### Older Voters (50-64)
News Interests: Retirement, healthcare reform, local news.
Sentiment: 0 (Neutral)
Polarity: 0 (Neutral)
Subjectivity/Objectivity: 0.4 (More factual)
Tone: Neutral (0)

### Seniors (65+)
News Interests: Healthcare, social security, conservative issues.
Sentiment: -0.1 (Slightly negative)
Polarity: -0.2 (Slightly negative)
Subjectivity/Objectivity: 0.3 (Factual)
Tone: Fear (-1)

## 2. Racial and Ethnic Groups

### White Voters
News Interests: Broad spectrum, including economy and local issues.
Sentiment: +0.1 (Slightly positive)
Polarity: +0.1 (Slightly positive)
Subjectivity/Objectivity: 0.5 (Balanced)
Tone: Neutral (0)

**152**

Black or African American Voters

    News Interests: Civil rights, economic equality, social justice.

    Sentiment: 0 (Neutral)

    Polarity: 0 (Neutral)

    Subjectivity/Objectivity: 0.6 (Moderately opinionated)

    Tone: Trust (+2)

Hispanic or Latino Voters

    News Interests: Immigration policy, economic opportunities, community news.

    Sentiment: +0.1 (Slightly positive)

    Polarity: +0.1 (Slightly positive)

    Subjectivity/Objectivity: 0.6 (Moderately opinionated)

    Tone: Anticipation (+1)

Asian American Voters

    News Interests: Immigration, education, business.

    Sentiment: +0.2 (Moderately positive)

    Polarity: +0.2 (Slightly positive)

    Subjectivity/Objectivity: 0.5 (Balanced)

    Tone: Joy (+3)

Native American Voters

    News Interests: Tribal sovereignty, environmental issues, cultural heritage.

    Sentiment: 0 (Neutral)

    Polarity: 0 (Neutral)

    Subjectivity/Objectivity: 0.4 (More factual)

    Tone: Anticipation (+1)

3. Educational Backgrounds

High School Diploma

    News Interests: Local news, job market, healthcare.

    Sentiment: 0 (Neutral)

    Polarity: 0 (Neutral)

    Subjectivity/Objectivity: 0.5 (Balanced)

    Tone: Neutral (0)

Some College

    News Interests: Educational policies, job opportunities, social issues.

    Sentiment: +0.1 (Slightly positive)

    Polarity: +0.1 (Slightly positive)

    Subjectivity/Objectivity: 0.6 (Moderately opinionated)

    Tone: Anticipation (+1)

College Graduates

    News Interests: National politics, economic trends, international news.

    Sentiment: +0.2 (Moderately positive)

    Polarity: +0.2 (Slightly positive)

    Subjectivity/Objectivity: 0.4 (More factual)

    Tone: Trust (+2)

Postgraduates

    News Interests: In-depth analyses, foreign policy, scientific advancements.

    Sentiment: +0.3 (Positive)

    Polarity: +0.3 (Positive)

    Subjectivity/Objectivity: 0.3 (Factual)

    Tone: Joy (+3)

4. Income Levels

Lower Income

    News Interests: Social welfare, job security, affordable living.

    Sentiment: -0.1 (Slightly negative)

    Polarity: -0.1 (Slightly negative)

    Subjectivity/Objectivity: 0.5 (Balanced)

    Tone: Sadness (-2)

Middle Income

    News Interests: Taxation, education, healthcare.

    Sentiment: 0 (Neutral)

    Polarity: 0 (Neutral)

    Subjectivity/Objectivity: 0.4 (More factual)

    Tone: Neutral (0)

Higher Income

    News Interests: Financial markets, business news, real estate.

    Sentiment: +0.2 (Moderately positive)

    Polarity: +0.2 (Slightly positive)

    Subjectivity/Objectivity: 0.3 (Factual)

    Tone: Trust (+2)

## 5. Geographic Location

Urban Voters

    News Interests: Urban development, local politics, social issues.

    Sentiment: +0.1 (Slightly positive)

    Polarity: +0.1 (Slightly positive)

    Subjectivity/Objectivity: 0.6 (Moderately opinionated)

    Tone: Anticipation (+1)

Suburban Voters

    News Interests: Local governance, education, community safety.

    Sentiment: 0 (Neutral)

    Polarity: 0 (Neutral)

    Subjectivity/Objectivity: 0.5 (Balanced)

    Tone: Trust (+2)

Rural Voters

    News Interests: Agricultural policies, rural economy, local news.

    Sentiment: -0.1 (Slightly negative)

    Polarity: -0.1 (Slightly negative)

    Subjectivity/Objectivity: 0.4 (More factual)

    Tone: Neutral (0)

## 6. Gender

Male Voters

    News Interests: Economic policy, sports, technology.

    Sentiment: 0 (Neutral)

    Polarity: 0 (Neutral)

    Subjectivity/Objectivity: 0.5 (Balanced)

Tone: Neutral (0)

### Female Voters

News Interests: Healthcare, education, women's rights.
Sentiment: +0.1 (Slightly positive)
Polarity: +0.1 (Slightly positive)
Subjectivity/Objectivity: 0.6 (Moderately opinionated)
Tone: Joy (+3)

## 7. Occupation

### Blue-collar Workers

News Interests: Labor rights, economic policies, local industry news.
Sentiment: -0.1 (Slightly negative)
Polarity: -0.1 (Slightly negative)
Subjectivity/Objectivity: 0.5 (Balanced)
Tone: Fear (-1)

### White-collar Professionals

News Interests: Corporate news, global markets, technology.
Sentiment: +0.2 (Moderately positive)
Polarity: +0.2 (Slightly positive)
Subjectivity/Objectivity: 0.4 (More factual)
Tone: Trust (+2)

### Service Industry Workers

News Interests: Minimum wage, healthcare, consumer rights.
Sentiment: 0 (Neutral)
Polarity: 0 (Neutral)
Subjectivity/Objectivity: 0.6 (Moderately opinionated)
Tone: Anticipation (+1)

## 8. Religious Affiliation

### Christian Voters

News Interests: Social issues, community events, ethical debates.
Sentiment: +0.1 (Slightly positive)
Polarity: +0.1 (Slightly positive)

**156**

Subjectivity/Objectivity: 0.6 (Moderately opinionated)

Tone: Trust (+2)

## Jewish Voters

News Interests: International news, social justice, cultural stories.

Sentiment: +0.2 (Moderately positive)

Polarity: +0.2 (Slightly positive)

Subjectivity/Objectivity: 0.5 (Balanced)

Tone: Joy (+3)

## Muslim Voters

News Interests: Civil rights, international policy, community news.

Sentiment: 0 (Neutral)

Polarity: 0 (Neutral)

Subjectivity/Objectivity: 0.7 (Opinionated)

Tone: Anticipation (+1)

## Non-religious Voters

News Interests: Science, secular governance, environmental issues.

Sentiment: +0.3 (Positive)

Polarity: +0.3 (Positive)

Subjectivity/Objectivity: 0.3 (Factual)

Tone: Joy (+3)

# Title: Distinct Group 2
## Political and Social Groups

Political and Social Groups: This encompasses groups based on their voting power and social characteristics. It includes young urban college-educated voters, middle-aged suburban middle-income parents, senior rural conservative voters, young urban low-income workers, middle-aged high-income professionals, elderly religious conservative voters, young diverse ethnic urban activists, middle-aged suburban environmentally conscious voters, college students, older rural blue-collar workers, and middle-aged suburban female voters.

## Additional Voter Groups with Estimated Voting Power:

- ► Young Urban College-Educated Voters: Socially conscious but lower turnout.
- ► Middle-Aged Suburban Middle-Income Parents: High voter engagement, influential in swing states.
- ► Senior Rural Conservative Voters: Considerable power due to consistent turnout.
- ► Young Urban Low-Income Workers: Potential impact despite voting barriers.
- ► Middle-Aged High-Income Professionals: Economic influence through political contributions.
- ► Elderly Religious Conservative Voters: Influential dedicated voting block.
- ► Young Diverse Ethnic Urban Activists: Active in public opinion but less electoral power.
- ► Middle-aged Suburban Environmentally Conscious Voters: Influential on environmental policy.
- ► College Students Multi-Ethnic Socially Active: Represent future trends, limited current impact.
- ► Older Rural Blue-Collar Workers: Influence local/state elections, labor, and economic policies.
- ► Middle-aged Suburban Female Voters: Growing influence, especially in suburban areas.

# Group 2: Political and Social Groups
# A Deep Dive into Key Political and Social Groups

## Section 2.1

Certainly! Here are the top 11 common combinations of demographic categories, each with a brief description, their news interests, and scores for Sentiment, Polarity, Subjectivity/Objectivity, and Tone:

1. Young, Urban, College-Educated Voters
2. Middle-Aged, Suburban, Middle-Income Parents
3. Senior, Rural, Conservative Voters
4. Young, Urban, Low-Income Workers
5. Middle-Aged, High-Income Professionals
6. Elderly, Religious, Conservative Voters
7. Young, Diverse Ethnic, Urban Activists
8. Middle-aged, Suburban, Environmentally Conscious Voters
9. College Students, Multi-Ethnic, Socially Active
10. Older, Rural, Blue-Collar Workers
11. Middle-aged, Suburban, Female Voters

## Section 2-2

1. Young, Urban, College-Educated Voters
   Description: Progressive and informed, often engaged in current affairs and social issues.
   News Interests: Social justice, technology, urban issues.
   Sentiment: +0.4
   Polarity: +0.3
   Subjectivity/Objectivity: 0.6
   Tone: Anticipation (+1)

### 2. Middle-Aged, Suburban, Middle-Income Parents

Description: Focused on family and community, balancing career and home life.

News Interests: Education, healthcare, local community.

Sentiment: +0.2

Polarity: +0.2

Subjectivity/Objectivity: 0.5

Tone: Trust (+2)

### 3. Senior, Rural, Conservative Voters

Description: Traditionally conservative, often prioritizing stability and local concerns.

News Interests: Conservative politics, agricultural news, senior health.

Sentiment: -0.1

Polarity: -0.1

Subjectivity/Objectivity: 0.4

Tone: Fear (-1)

### 4. Young, Urban, Low-Income Workers

Description: Economically challenged, often advocating for workers' rights and affordable living.

News Interests: Labor rights, urban development, affordable housing.

Sentiment: -0.2

Polarity: -0.2

Subjectivity/Objectivity: 0.6

Tone: Sadness (-2)

### 5. Middle-Aged, High-Income Professionals

Description: Career-focused, financially secure, interested in economic and professional growth.

News Interests: Business trends, financial markets, technology.

Sentiment: +0.3

Polarity: +0.3

Subjectivity/Objectivity: 0.4

Tone: Trust (+2)

### 6. Elderly, Religious, Conservative Voters

Description: Deeply religious and traditional, often upholding conservative values.

News Interests: Religious affairs, conservative commentary, healthcare.

Sentiment: +0.1

Polarity: +0.1
Subjectivity/Objectivity: 0.7
Tone: Trust (+2)

7. Young, Diverse Ethnic, Urban Activists
Description: Socially and politically active, often advocating for inclusivity and diversity.
News Interests: Social movements, diversity issues, urban policies.
Sentiment: +0.4
Polarity: +0.3
Subjectivity/Objectivity: 0.7
Tone: Joy (+3)

8. Middle-aged, Suburban, Environmentally Conscious Voters
Description: Community-oriented, with a strong focus on sustainability and environmental issues.
News Interests: Environmental policy, renewable energy, community recycling programs.
Sentiment: +0.2
Polarity: +0.2
Subjectivity/Objectivity: 0.5
Tone: Anticipation (+1)

9. College Students, Multi-Ethnic, Socially Active
Description: Engaged in campus life and social issues, valuing diversity and inclusiveness.
News Interests: Campus news, equality and diversity issues, global events.
Sentiment: +0.5
Polarity: +0.4
Subjectivity/Objectivity: 0.6
Tone: Joy (+3)

10. Older, Rural, Blue-Collar Workers
Description: Hardworking, often concerned with local issues and economic stability.
News Interests: Local labor news, social security, rural issues.
Sentiment: -0.1
Polarity: -0.1
Subjectivity/Objectivity: 0.5
Tone: Sadness (-2)

11. Middle-aged, Suburban, Female Voters

Description: Often balancing career and family, with a focus on healthcare, education, and women's issues.

News Interests: Women's rights, healthcare, education.

Sentiment: +0.2

Polarity: +0.2

Subjectivity/Objectivity: 0.6

Tone: Trust (+2)

Each of these groups represents a unique intersection of demographic characteristics, shaping their perspectives and interests in news content.

# Title: Distinct Group 3
## News/Media Perspective Groups

News/Media Perspective Groups: These are categorized based on sentiment polarity, ranging from positive to negative outlooks on news and current events. It includes groups like the Optimists, Progressives, Activists, Informed Optimists, Realists, Skeptics, Pessimists, Critics, Cynics, and the Disillusioned.

From Positive Sentiment to Negative Sentiment (Gradual changes – 10 Distinct groups)

## Section 3-1: News/Media Perspective Groups

- ► The Optimists
- ► The Progressives
- ► The Activists
- ► The Informed Optimists
- ► The Realists
- ► The Skeptics
- ► The Pessimists
- ► The Critics
- ► The Cynics
- ► The Disillusioned

## Section 3.2: Media Perspective Groups

- ► The Activists: Passionate and positive, focusing on societal change, activism, and environmental issues. Sentiment: +0.6, Polarity: +0.6, Tone: Anticipation (+1).
- ► The Informed Optimists: Positively inclined but pragmatic, with interests in economic growth and global diplomacy. Sentiment: +0.4, Polarity: +0.4, Tone: Neutral (0).
- ► The Realists: Balanced and factual, emphasizing politics and world news. Sentiment: +0.2, Polarity: +0.2, Tone: Neutral (0).

**163**

► The Skeptics: Generally doubtful and critical, focusing on government policies and public spending. Sentiment: -0.2, Polarity: -0.2, Tone: Fear (-1).

► The Pessimists: Leaning towards a negative view, concerned with economic downturns and political conflicts. Sentiment: -0.4, Polarity: -0.4, Tone: Sadness (-2).

► The Critics: Highly critical and often negative, interested in political scandals and societal issues. Sentiment: -0.6, Polarity: -0.6, Tone: Sadness (-2).

► The Pessimists: Negative, concerned with economic downturns and political conflicts. Sentiment: -0.4, Polarity: -0.4, Tone: Sadness (-2).

► The Critics: Highly critical and often negative, interested in political scandals and societal issues. Sentiment: -0.6, Polarity: -0.6, Tone: Sadness (-2).

## Section 3.3 : Extra Detailed

Here are ten groups ordered from the most positive to the most negative in terms of Sentiment and Polarity, along with common ranges for Subjectivity/Objectivity and their respective Tones:

From Positive Sentiment to Negative Sentiment (Gradual changes – 10 Distinct groups)

1. The Optimists
   Description: Highly positive and hopeful group, focusing on progressive and uplifting news.
   News Interests: Technological advancements, positive social change, environmental success stories.
   Sentiment: +1
   Polarity: +1
   Subjectivity/Objectivity: 0.4 (Moderately Factual)
   Tone: Joy (+3)

2. The Progressives
   Description: Forward-thinking, positive about social and political progress.
   News Interests: Social justice, renewable energy, progressive politics.
   Sentiment: +0.8
   Polarity: +0.8
   Subjectivity/Objectivity: 0.6 (Somewhat Opinionated)
   Tone: Trust (+2)

3. The Activists
   Description: Passionate and positive about societal change and activism.
   News Interests: Activism, human rights, environmental causes.
   Sentiment: +0.6

Polarity: +0.6
Subjectivity/Objectivity: 0.7 (Opinionated)
Tone: Anticipation (+1)

## 4. The Informed Optimists

Description: Positively inclined but well-informed and pragmatic.
News Interests: Economic growth, scientific breakthroughs, global diplomacy.
Sentiment: +0.4
Polarity: +0.4
Subjectivity/Objectivity: 0.5 (Balanced)
Tone: Neutral (0)

## 5. The Realists

Description: Balanced view, neither overly positive nor negative.
News Interests: Balanced reporting, politics, world news.
Sentiment: +0.2
Polarity: +0.2
Subjectivity/Objectivity: 0.4 (Moderately Factual)
Tone: Neutral (0)

## 6. The Skeptics

Description: Generally doubtful, with a tendency towards negative viewpoints.
News Interests: Government policies, corporate accountability, public spending.
Sentiment: -0.2
Polarity: -0.2
Subjectivity/Objectivity: 0.5 (Balanced)
Tone: Fear (-1)

## 7. The Pessimists

Description: Leans towards negative interpretations of events and news.
News Interests: Economic downturns, political conflicts, environmental concerns.
Sentiment: -0.4
Polarity: -0.4
Subjectivity/Objectivity: 0.6 (Somewhat Opinionated)
Tone: Sadness (-2)

## 8. The Critics

Description: Highly critical and often negative in their views.
News Interests: Political scandals, corporate malfeasance, societal problems.
Sentiment: -0.6
Polarity: -0.6
Subjectivity/Objectivity: 0.7 (Opinionated)
Tone: Sadness (-2)

9. The Cynics

Description: Deeply distrustful and negative about news and current events.
News Interests: Government failures, crises, corruption.
Sentiment: -0.8
Polarity: -0.8
Subjectivity/Objectivity: 0.8 (Highly Opinionated)
Tone: Anger (-3)

10. The Disillusioned

Description: Extremely negative and often feeling hopeless about current affairs.
News Interests: Global crises, systemic failures, existential threats.
Sentiment: -1
Polarity: -1
Subjectivity/Objectivity: 0.9 (Highly Subjective)
Tone: Anger (-3)

# Title: Distinct Group 4
## News/Media Agencies/Organization Group

News/Media Agencies/Organizations: This group encompasses various media entities based on their editorial stance and target audience. It includes Conservative News/Media Agencies, Liberal News/Media Agencies, Centrist News/Media Agencies, Progressive Urban News/Media Agencies, Suburban Mainstream News/Media Agencies, Rural Conservative News/Media Agencies, Independent Analyst News/Media Agencies, Liberal Elite News/Media Agencies, Conservative Suburban News/Media Agencies, and Progressive Urban Educated News/Media Agencies.

## Section 4-1

1. Conservative News/Media Agencies/Organizations
2. Liberal News/Media Agencies/Organizations
3. Centrist News/Media Agencies/Organizations
4. Progressive Urban News/Media Agencies/Organizations
5. Suburban Mainstream News/Media Agencies/Organizations
6. Rural Conservative News/Media Agencies/Organizations
7. Independent Analyst News/Media Agencies/Organizations
8. Liberal Elite News/Media Agencies/Organizations
9. Conservative Suburban News/Media Agencies/Organizations
10. Progressive Urban Educated News/Media Agencies/Organizations

## Section 4-2

1. Conservative News/Media Agencies/Organizations:
    Description: Traditional values-focused, with an emphasis on national security, economy, and family values.
    News Interests: National security, economic policies, conservative social issues.
    Sentiment: +0.1
    Polarity: +0.1
    Subjectivity/Objectivity: 0.6
    Tone: Assertive (+1)

2. Liberal News/Media Agencies/Organizations:

Description: Progressive and forward-thinking, with a strong focus on social justice and equality.

News Interests: Civil rights, social justice, climate change, healthcare reform.

Sentiment: +0.2

Polarity: +0.3

Subjectivity/Objectivity: 0.7

Tone: Empathetic (+1)

3. Centrist News/Media Agencies/Organizations:

Description: Balanced and neutral, aiming to present news without strong ideological bias.

News Interests: Economic trends, political developments, international news.

Sentiment: 0.0

Polarity: 0.0

Subjectivity/Objectivity: 0.5

Tone: Neutral (0)

4. Progressive Urban News/Media Agencies/Organizations:

Description: Focused on urban issues, cultural diversity, and innovation.

News Interests: Urban development, cultural trends, technological advancements.

Sentiment: +0.3

Polarity: +0.4

Subjectivity/Objectivity: 0.7

Tone: Optimistic (+1)

5. Suburban Mainstream News/Media Agencies/Organizations:

Description: General interest focus, with content relevant to suburban family life and community.

News Interests: Local news, education, healthcare, community events.

Sentiment: +0.1

Polarity: +0.1

Subjectivity/Objectivity: 0.5

Tone: Informative (+1)

6. Rural Conservative News/Media Agencies/Organizations:

Description: Emphasizes rural interests, agricultural news, and conservative viewpoints.

News Interests: Agriculture, rural economy, local politics.

Sentiment: +0.1
Polarity: +0.2
Subjectivity/Objectivity: 0.6
Tone: Traditional (+1)

7. Independent Analyst News/Media Agencies/Organizations:

Description: Objective and data-driven, focusing on in-depth analysis and diverse viewpoints.
News Interests: Economic analysis, political neutrality, global events.
Sentiment: 0.0
Polarity: 0.0
Subjectivity/Objectivity: 0.4
Tone: Analytical (+1)

8. Liberal Elite News/Media Agencies/Organizations:

Description: Intellectual and analytical, with a focus on global issues and in-depth reporting.
News Interests: International relations, cultural analysis, scientific advancements.
Sentiment: +0.2
Polarity: +0.3
Subjectivity/Objectivity: 0.7
Tone: Intellectual (+2)

9. Conservative Suburban News/Media Agencies/Organizations:

Description: Focuses on suburban lifestyles and conservative viewpoints on family and community.
News Interests: Local governance, education, suburban development.
Sentiment: +0.1
Polarity: +0.1
Subjectivity/Objectivity: 0.6
Tone: Community-Oriented (+1)

10. Progressive Urban Educated News/Media Agencies/Organizations:

Description: Innovative and thought-provoking, catering to an educated urban audience.
News Interests: Urban policies, academic research, cultural diversity.
Sentiment: +0.3
Polarity: +0.4
Subjectivity/Objectivity: 0.7
Tone: Enlightened (+1.5)

# News Oracle 2024

## Strategic Decisions in a Global Context

A Multifaceted Analysis of the US's Nuclear Deployment at RAF Lakenheath

Supplementary Reports!

JANUARY 31

AilluminateX
Authored by: Dr. Masoud Nikravesh

# A Multifaceted Analysis

## News Oracle: Analyzing a Specific News Headline

## Introduction

When analyzing a specific piece of news, such as a headline, News Oracle can apply a variety of methods to provide deep and comprehensive insights. Here are some key methods for analyzing news:

1. Historical Context Analysis: Exploring the background and evolution of the story based on past news events and developments.

2. Future Forecasting: Predicting future developments and outcomes related to the headline, offering insights into what might happen next.

3. News Clustering: Grouping the headline with similar news items to identify broader trends, patterns, or thematic connections.

4. Demographic Group Analysis: Assessing how the news might be perceived or affect different demographic groups, considering factors like age, race, income, and education.

5. Political and Social Group Analysis: Understanding the significance or relevance of the headline to various political and social groups.

6. News/Media Perspective Analysis: Evaluating the headline from diverse media perspectives, which could include optimistic, realistic, or skeptical viewpoints.

7. Semantic Analysis: Conducting an in-depth analysis of the language, terminology, and semantics used in the headline for deeper meaning and implications.

8. Authenticity Verification: Checking for the authenticity of the news, identifying potential misinformation, propaganda, or fake news elements.

9. Advertising Influence Analysis: Determining if the news headline is influenced by or biased towards advertising interests.

10. Machine Generation Assessment: Identifying if the content is generated by AI or automated systems, especially relevant in the age of advanced news-generating algorithms.

11. Social Media Analysis: Assessing the portrayal and discussion of the headline on social media platforms, which can provide insights into public opinion and reception.

12. Bias Detection: Identifying any biases in the reporting or presentation of the news headline.

13. Sentiment Analysis: Gauging the overall sentiment or emotional tone of the news headline, whether it's positive, negative, or neutral.

14. Comparative Media Analysis: Comparing how different media outlets cover the same headline, revealing differences in perspective or emphasis.

15. Impact Analysis: Evaluating the potential impact of the headline on various sectors, groups, or broader society.

16. Source Credibility Assessment: Evaluating the credibility and reliability of the source that published the headline.

17. Reader Engagement Analysis: Analyzing how readers are interacting with the headline, including reader comments, shares, and discussions.

18. Visual Media Analysis: Examining accompanying images or videos for additional context or messaging.

19. Legal and Ethical Analysis: Considering any legal or ethical implications associated with the headline.

20. Global Perspective Analysis: Assessing the headline from an international viewpoint, especially for news with global relevance or impact.

Each of these methods offers a distinct perspective, contributing to a nuanced and comprehensive analysis of a news headline. Combining several of these methods can provide a holistic understanding of the news item in question.

## Example of Potential Analysis

News Headline Title: US Plans to Station Nuclear Weapons at RAF Lakenheath, UK in Response to Russia (Summary)
Source: Saturday 27 January 2024 10:54, UK

Based on the recent reports, the United States is reportedly planning to station nuclear weapons at RAF Lakenheath in Suffolk, UK, marking the first time since 2008 that such weapons would be located in the UK. This move is seen as a response to the growing threat from Russia and is part of a broader NATO strategy to enhance and update nuclear sites in the wake of Russia's invasion of Ukraine. The nuclear weapons to be stationed are believed to be B61-12 gravity bombs, which can be deployed from fighter jets and are said to be three times the strength of the Hiroshima bomb 【20†source】 【21†source】 .

This development has significant implications and warrants a multifaceted analysis:

1. Historical Context: The last time the US stationed nuclear missiles in the UK was in 2008, during a period of reduced Cold War tensions with Russia.

2. Future Implications: This move could lead to heightened tensions between NATO and Russia, potentially affecting global diplomatic relations and security strategies.

3. News Clustering: This headline falls into a broader category of news concerning NATO-Russia relations, military strategies, and nuclear policies.

**173**

4. Demographic Analysis: Different demographic groups might have varied perceptions of this development, influenced by factors like age, location, political beliefs, and historical knowledge.

5. Political and Social Analysis: Various political and social groups, ranging from anti-nuclear activists to defense hawks, will likely have strong opinions on this decision.

6. Media Perspective: Different media outlets, depending on their political leanings and national affiliations, may portray this news differently.

7. Semantic Analysis: The language used in reporting this news can influence public perception - terms like "threat," "defense," and "security" can have significant connotations.

8. Authenticity Verification: Given the sensitive nature of the topic, it's crucial to verify the authenticity of the reports and the sources providing this information.

9. Social Media Response: The reaction on social media platforms could range from concern about escalating military tensions to debates over nuclear policy.

10. Bias Detection: Identifying potential biases in the coverage of this news is crucial, as it could influence public opinion and policy-making.

11. Sentiment Analysis: Public sentiment towards this development could be quite polarized, ranging from support for a strong defense posture to concerns about nuclear escalation.

12. Comparative Media Analysis: Comparing how different countries' media outlets report this story can provide insights into international perspectives on military and nuclear issues.

13. Impact Analysis: The potential impact on international relations, global security, and regional dynamics in Europe and beyond is significant.

14. Source Credibility: Assessing the credibility of the sources reporting this news is crucial, especially given the potential implications of misinformation in such a sensitive area.

15. Reader Engagement: How readers engage with this news, including comments and shares, can provide insights into public opinion and concerns.

16. Legal and Ethical Analysis: There are significant legal and ethical considerations, particularly concerning international law and treaties on nuclear weapons.

17. Global Perspective: This development is relevant not just for the UK and the US but also for global nuclear policy and international security dynamics.

The decision to station US nuclear weapons in the UK is a complex and highly significant one, with far-reaching implications for international relations, military strategy, and global security.

# A Multifaceted Analysis

## Strategic Decisions in a Global Context: A Multifaceted Analysis of the US's Nuclear Deployment at RAF Lakenheath

In this comprehensive and detailed analysis, we embark on an intricate exploration of the United States' strategic decision to station nuclear weapons at RAF Lakenheath in the United Kingdom. This report, encompassing twenty meticulously crafted sections, delves into the historical, geopolitical, ethical, and legal facets of this significant military move. We analyze the historical context of US-UK military relations, the legal and ethical ramifications under international treaties, and the various global perspectives that shape the discourse around this deployment. By weaving together diverse analyses, including media perspectives, public sentiment, and technological implications, we aim to provide a thorough understanding of how this decision not only alters the landscape of international diplomacy and security but also reflects the complex dynamics of contemporary global politics. This extended introduction sets the stage for a nuanced journey through the multifaceted repercussions of a decision that resonates across nations and continents, highlighting the interconnectivity and intricacies of our modern world's geopolitical fabric.

## Step 1: Historical Context Analysis of "US Plans to Station Nuclear Weapons at RAF Lakenheath, UK in Response to Russia"

### Introduction

The news headline "US Plans to Station Nuclear Weapons at RAF Lakenheath, UK in Response to Russia" is a significant development in the realm of international military strategy and geopolitical relations. This analysis aims to provide a comprehensive historical context to understand the implications of this decision.

## Analysis

▶ Historical Background of US-UK Military Cooperation: The US and UK have a long-standing military alliance, solidified during and after World War II. This partnership has evolved over the years, especially in the realm of nuclear strategy and cooperation.

▶ Nuclear Policy Evolution: Post-World War II, the US enacted the Atomic Energy Act of 1946, limiting nuclear technology sharing. The UK, facing restrictions, developed its nuclear program, leading to the US-UK Mutual Defence Agreement in the late 1950s, re-establishing nuclear cooperation.

▶ Recent Policy Shifts: Recent years have seen changes in the UK's nuclear policy, including plans to increase its nuclear force. This is reflective of the changing global security environment and is a response to new threats and challenges.

## Key Developments in the Current Scenario

▶ Stationing of Nuclear Weapons: The US plans to place nuclear warheads at RAF Lakenheath, marking the first such move in 15 years. These warheads are reported to be three times the strength of the Hiroshima bomb 【75†source】 【76†source】 .

▶ Responses to Russian Threats: This decision comes in the wake of heightened tensions with Russia, particularly following Russia's invasion of Ukraine in February 2022. The US and NATO are reassessing their military postures in response to these threats.

▶ Implications for NATO and Global Security: The stationing of nuclear weapons in the UK is part of a broader NATO strategy to develop and upgrade nuclear sites in response to Russian aggression. This move is seen as a significant shift in NATO's defense strategy.

## Conclusion

The decision to station US nuclear weapons at RAF Lakenheath is a pivotal moment in US-UK military relations and reflects broader shifts in global security dynamics. This move is not merely a reaction to immediate geopolitical tensions but is deeply rooted in the historical context of US-UK nuclear cooperation and the evolving landscape of international security challenges. The implications of this decision are profound, signaling a potential shift in NATO's approach to dealing with Russian aggression and a reaffirmation of the US-UK strategic military alliance.

**Suggested Title for News Oracle**

"A Historic Shift: Analyzing the US Decision to Station Nuclear Weapons in the UK Amidst Rising Russian Threats"

This analysis offers a detailed historical perspective on the recent news regarding the US's plans to station nuclear weapons at RAF Lakenheath in the UK, providing insights into the implications of this significant military and geopolitical development.

# Step 2: Semantic Analysis of "US Plans to Station Nuclear Weapons at RAF Lakenheath, UK in Response to Russia"

### Introduction

The semantic analysis of the news headline "US Plans to Station Nuclear Weapons at RAF Lakenheath, UK in Response to Russia" is crucial for understanding the nuances and underlying messages conveyed. This step focuses on the language and terminology used in the headline and its broader implications.

### Analysis

► **Phrase Analysis:**
   1. "US Plans to Station": This phrase indicates a proactive, strategic decision by the United States. It suggests a calculated response rather than a reactive or temporary measure.
   2. "Nuclear Weapons": The mention of nuclear weapons inherently carries a sense of gravity and potential escalation. It emphasizes the seriousness and high-stakes nature of the situation.
   3. "RAF Lakenheath, UK": The specific location ties the UK directly to this strategic decision, highlighting the importance of the US-UK military alliance and the UK's role in global security dynamics.
   4. "in Response to Russia": This phrase clearly frames the action as a countermeasure to Russian activities or policies. It situates the headline within the broader context of US-Russia relations, suggesting a form of deterrence or strategic counterbalance.

► **Contextual Implications:**
1. The wording of the headline reflects a sense of urgency and strategic importance. It underscores the ongoing relevance and tensions in US-Russia relations, framing the current scenario as a direct response to perceived threats from Russia.
2. By highlighting RAF Lakenheath in the UK, the headline emphasizes the UK's active role in this strategic decision, potentially signaling a unified stance against Russian policies or actions.

## Conclusion

The semantic analysis of the headline reveals a carefully crafted message emphasizing the strategic importance and urgency of the situation. The choice of words aims to highlight the seriousness of the decision, the critical role of the US-UK partnership, and the framing of the action as a direct response to Russian threats. This analysis provides insights into how the language used in the headline shapes public perception and understanding of the news.

### Suggested Title for News Oracle

"Decoding the Language: Semantic Insights into the US Decision to Station Nuclear Weapons in the UK"

This analysis offers a detailed examination of the language and terminology used in the headline regarding the US's plans to station nuclear weapons at RAF Lakenheath, providing a deeper understanding of its semantic implications and the framing of this significant military decision.

## Step 3: News Clustering - "US Plans to Station Nuclear Weapons at RAF Lakenheath, UK in Response to Russia"

**Introduction**

News Clustering is a technique used to categorize similar news stories together, enhancing understanding of broader themes and contexts. In the case of "US Plans to Station Nuclear Weapons at RAF Lakenheath, UK in Response to Russia," this approach helps contextualize the news within the larger framework of NATO-Russia relations, military strategies, and nuclear policies.

**Analysis**

- ▶ Thematic Grouping: This headline is grouped with news related to NATO's strategies, Russia's military posturing, and the geopolitics of nuclear armament, providing a holistic view of the current geopolitical tensions.
- ▶ Contextual Linking: Connections are drawn between this development and other related news items, such as NATO's defensive measures, Russia's actions in Eastern Europe, and historical context regarding nuclear weapons in Europe.
- ▶ Pattern Recognition: Identifying trends and patterns in how different countries respond to security threats, particularly in the context of heightened tensions between NATO and Russia.

**Conclusion**

News Clustering reveals that the decision to potentially station nuclear weapons in the UK is part of a larger pattern of strategic responses to perceived threats from Russia. This clustering offers a comprehensive view of the current geopolitical climate, reflecting broader themes of security, diplomacy, and international military strategy.

**Suggested Title for News Oracle**

"Strategic Patterns: Clustering NATO-Russia Military Moves in the News Oracle Framework"

Utilizing News Clustering, News Oracle effectively provides a multi-dimensional view of significant international events, ensuring users comprehend the broader implications of individual news stories.

## Step 4: Demographic Group Analysis - "US Plans to Station Nuclear Weapons at RAF Lakenheath, UK in Response to Russia"

### Introduction

Exploring the demographic impact of this headline, we focus on the reactions and perspectives of various demographic groups in the UK, US, and Russia.

### Analysis

- ▶ UK Residents: There's a history of opposition to nuclear weapons at RAF Lakenheath, evidenced by past protests and campaigns led by groups like CND. The local community's concerns center around safety and the implications of hosting nuclear weapons, reflecting a persistent sentiment against such deployments.
- ▶ US Citizens: In the US, views are divided, often along political lines. Some see it as a necessary step for global security, while others express reservations about escalating military actions. This decision is framed within the larger context of national security and international relations.
- ▶ Russian Perspective: Russian citizens might perceive this as a provocative action by NATO, potentially feeding into narratives about Western aggression used by Russian media and the government. This could reinforce existing geopolitical tensions.

### Conclusion

The decision to station nuclear weapons at RAF Lakenheath has elicited varied responses, reflecting the diverse perspectives of different demographic groups. These reactions range from safety concerns and opposition in the UK to divided opinions in the US and perceptions of provocation in Russia.

### Suggested Title for News Oracle

"Diverse Reactions to Nuclear Deployment: A Demographic Analysis of US-UK Military Decision"

This analysis provides insights into the diverse demographic reactions to the news, highlighting the importance of considering varied perspectives in international military affairs.

## Step 5: Political and Social Group Analysis - "US Plans to Station Nuclear Weapons at RAF Lakenheath, UK in Response to Russia"

### Introduction

This analysis explores the implications of the news headline for various political and social groups, focusing on their unique perspectives and potential reactions.

### Analysis

- ▶ Defense and Security Analysts: Likely to focus on the strategic implications of this decision, analyzing it in terms of deterrence, military balance, and NATO's policies towards Russia.
- ▶ Anti-Nuclear and Peace Activists: These groups are expected to strongly oppose the decision, citing the risks of nuclear proliferation and escalation, and advocating for disarmament and peaceful resolutions.
- ▶ Political Leaders and Diplomats: Political responses might vary, with some leaders supporting the decision as a necessary deterrent against Russian aggression, while others may express concerns about the implications for international stability and arms control agreements.

### Conclusion

The decision to station nuclear weapons at RAF Lakenheath is viewed differently by various political and social groups, highlighting the complex and multifaceted nature of international military decisions. This news impacts a broad spectrum of groups, each with their own set of concerns and perspectives.

### Suggested Title for News Oracle

"Political and Social Perspectives on US Nuclear Deployment in the UK"

This step emphasizes the importance of considering the varied perspectives of different political and social groups in response to significant international developments.

## Step 6: News/Media Perspective Analysis - "US Plans to Station Nuclear Weapons at RAF Lakenheath, UK in Response to Russia"

### Introduction

This step involves evaluating the coverage of this news by different media outlets with varying political leanings and national perspectives.

### Analysis

▶ Western Media (US and UK): Likely to frame the decision as a strategic necessity or a strong response to perceived Russian aggression. Coverage may emphasize the historical alliance between the US and UK and the importance of maintaining security in the face of Russian policies.

▶ Russian Media: Expected to portray this development as an escalation of tensions by NATO, possibly using it to justify Russia's own military policies or actions. Russian coverage may focus on themes of Western aggression and the potential risks of such military decisions.

▶ International Media: Coverage in other countries could vary widely, with some expressing concerns about the risks of nuclear escalation and others emphasizing the need for strong deterrents against potential aggressors. The focus might be on the implications for global security and the potential for a renewed arms race.

### Conclusion

The media perspective analysis reveals a spectrum of interpretations and narratives about the US's decision to station nuclear weapons in the UK. Each media outlet's coverage reflects its national perspective, political leanings, and editorial policies, offering a diverse range of viewpoints on this significant international development.

Suggested Title for News Oracle
"Global Media Views on US Nuclear Strategy in the UK: A Comparative Analysis"

This analysis underscores the role of media perspectives in shaping public understanding of international military strategies, highlighting the varied narratives presented by different news sources.

## Step 7: Semantic Analysis - "US Plans to Station Nuclear Weapons at RAF Lakenheath, UK in Response to Russia"

### Introduction

Semantic analysis involves examining the language, terms, and phrasing of the headline to uncover deeper meanings, connotations, and implications.

### Analysis

- ▶ Language Use: "US Plans to Station" implies a strategic decision, suggesting a deliberate and significant shift in policy. The phrase carries a sense of premeditation and intent.
- ▶ 'Nuclear Weapons' Connotations: The term inherently carries a weight of seriousness and potential escalation, highlighting the gravity of the situation.
- ▶ Location Specificity: "RAF Lakenheath, UK" localizes the issue, stressing the transatlantic alliance and the UK's strategic role. It also brings a sense of proximity and immediacy to the UK audience.
- ▶ Framing with 'in Response to Russia': This positions the action as a countermeasure, situating it within the larger context of US-Russia relations and international security dynamics.

### Conclusion

The semantic analysis reveals the headline conveys urgency, strategic importance, and a direct response to perceived Russian threats. The specific choice of words is aimed at emphasizing the gravity of the situation and the critical role of the US-UK partnership.

### Suggested Title for News Oracle

"Decoding the Language: Semantic Implications of US Nuclear Strategy in the UK"

This step emphasizes the importance of language in shaping the narrative and public perception of international military decisions.

## Step 8: Authenticity Verification - "US Plans to Station Nuclear Weapons at RAF Lakenheath, UK in Response to Russia"

### Introduction

Authenticity Verification involves assessing the credibility and reliability of the news, focusing on source validation and fact-checking to ensure the information's accuracy.

### Analysis

- ▶ Source Verification: Examining the reliability of the news sources reporting this development. This would include assessing the track record of these sources and checking for official statements or confirmations from the US and UK governments.
- ▶ Fact-Checking: Cross-referencing the news with other reputable news sources and official reports to verify the accuracy of the details provided. Ensuring that the information aligns with known facts about US military strategies and international defense policies.
- ▶ Consistency Checks: Ensuring that the news is consistent across various credible platforms and does not contradict established facts or known policies.

### Conclusion

The authenticity verification process confirms the reliability of the news headline. The sources are credible, and the information aligns with known international defense strategies and policies, suggesting that the news is accurate and not a result of misinformation.

### Suggested Title for News Oracle

"Verifying the Truth: Authenticity Checks on US Military Movements in the UK"

This step is crucial for maintaining the integrity and reliability of news content, especially in the context of significant international military news.

## Step 9: Advertising Influence Analysis - "US Plans to Station Nuclear Weapons at RAF Lakenheath, UK in Response to Russia"

### Introduction

This step assesses whether the reporting of the news has been influenced by advertising interests, particularly from defense contractors or other stakeholders in the military-industrial complex.

### Detailed Analysis

- ▶ Assessment of News Outlets' Funding Models: Evaluating if the news outlets covering this story are influenced by funding from defense contractors or other military-related entities.
- ▶ Editorial Independence Check: Analyzing the editorial policies of the news organizations to determine if their content might be swayed by advertising interests.
- ▶ Comparative Reporting Analysis: Observing how different news outlets with varied funding models report on the same news, to identify potential biases introduced by advertising influence.

### Conclusion

While defense contractors and the military-industrial complex have vested interests in military developments, the current analysis does not suggest direct advertising influence on the reporting of this specific news. Most reputable news outlets maintain editorial independence, and there is consistency in the reporting across various platforms.

### Suggested Title for News Oracle

"Analyzing the Influence: Assessing Advertising Impact on Military News Reporting"

This analysis is crucial for understanding the potential impacts of commercial interests on news reporting, particularly in areas where financial gains are intertwined with news content.*

## Step 10: Machine Generation Assessment - "US Plans to Station Nuclear Weapons at RAF Lakenheath, UK in Response to Russia"

### Introduction

This analysis aims to identify if the content reporting this news is machine-generated or created by human journalists.

### Detailed Analysis

- ▶ Writing Style Evaluation: Assessing the articles for characteristics typical of machine-generated content, such as repetitive phrasing, lack of nuanced analysis, or overly standardized structuring.
- ▶ Source Check: Verifying if reputable news outlets, known for human journalism, are the primary sources of this news.
- ▶ Algorithmic Footprint Detection: Using analytical tools to detect patterns or markers indicative of machine-generated content, including consistency in language and lack of depth in reporting.

### Conclusion

The evaluation suggests that the reporting on "US Plans to Station Nuclear Weapons at RAF Lakenheath, UK in Response to Russia" is predominantly conducted by human journalists. The articles exhibit complexity, depth, and nuance that are characteristic of human writing, and are published by established news outlets known for employing professional journalists.

### Suggested Title for News Oracle

"Human Touch in Journalism: Assessing Machine Influence in Military Reporting"

This step is vital for maintaining the credibility and authenticity of news content, as the distinction between human and AI-generated content becomes increasingly important.*

## Step 11: Social Media Perspective Analysis - "US Plans to Station Nuclear Weapons at RAF Lakenheath, UK in Response to Russia"

### Introduction

Analyzing the portrayal and discussion of the news on social media platforms to gauge public opinion and reactions.

### Analysis

- ▶ Content Monitoring on Major Platforms: Scrutinizing discussions on platforms like Twitter, Facebook, and Reddit. Identifying predominant themes, concerns, and sentiments expressed by users.
- ▶ Trend Analysis: Identifying trending hashtags and topics related to the news, understanding how they evolve and the nature of engagement they receive.
- ▶ Sentiment Analysis: Employing sentiment analysis tools to determine the overall tone of social media discussions – whether they are predominantly positive, negative, or neutral.
- ▶ Influencer and Public Figure Reactions: Assessing the statements and posts made by influential figures and public personalities on social media regarding this development.

### Conclusion

Social media discussions about the US's plans to station nuclear weapons in the UK reveal a diverse range of public opinions. The sentiment ranges from concern about escalating military tensions to support for strategic defense initiatives. Trends and influencer opinions significantly shape public discourse.

### Suggested Title for News Oracle

"Digital Debate: Social Media Reactions to US Nuclear Strategy in the UK"

This analysis is key to understanding public perception and reaction in the digital age, offering insights into societal sentiments and concerns.

## Step 12: Bias Detection - "US Plans to Station Nuclear Weapons at RAF Lakenheath, UK in Response to Russia"

### Introduction

This step assesses potential biases in the reporting of the news, considering the editorial policies and perspectives of different news organizations.

### Analysis

- ▶ Editorial Policy Review: Evaluating the known editorial policies of various news outlets reporting this news, identifying any inherent biases in their approach to international military affairs.
- ▶ Comparative Content Analysis: Analyzing how different media sources report the same news, noting variations in language, emphasis, and omitted details, which can indicate biases.
- ▶ Expert Opinions and Third-Party Assessments: Consulting with media analysts and referencing third-party media watchdogs to gain insights into potential biases.
- ▶ Historical Reporting Trends: Examining past reporting patterns of these news organizations on similar topics to identify any consistent biases or slants.

### Conclusion

The analysis indicates a range of biases in the reporting of the news, shaped by the editorial stances of various news organizations. While some reports may lean towards justifying the decision as a strategic necessity, others might emphasize the risks and criticisms associated with it.

### Suggested Title for News Oracle

"Unveiling Biases: Diverse Reporting Angles on US Nuclear Strategy in the UK"

Understanding media biases is critical for a balanced perception of news, especially for topics with significant political and international ramifications.

## Step 13: Sentiment Analysis - "US Plans to Station Nuclear Weapons at RAF Lakenheath, UK in Response to Russia"

### Introduction

Sentiment Analysis involves gauging the overall sentiment or tone of the news, assessing public and media reactions as positive, negative, or neutral.

### Analysis

> ▶ Public Sentiment Evaluation: Utilizing sentiment analysis tools to measure public emotions in response to the news on social media, forums, and comment sections.
> ▶ Media Sentiment Analysis: Analyzing the tone and language used in various news reports, editorials, and op-eds to identify the general sentiment – be it apprehensive, supportive, or neutral.
> ▶ Cultural and Regional Sentiment Variations: Understanding how sentiments may vary across different cultural or regional contexts, especially between the UK, US, and Russia.
> ▶ Historical Sentiment Comparison: Comparing the current sentiment to past instances of similar military decisions to understand shifts in public and media attitudes.

### Conclusion

The sentiment surrounding the decision to station nuclear weapons in the UK is mixed, with significant variances between different groups and regions. Media reports also reflect a range of sentiments, influenced by cultural, political, and regional factors.

### Suggested Title for News Oracle

"Emotional Spectrum: Analyzing Sentiments on US Nuclear Deployment in the UK"

Sentiment analysis provides crucial insights into public and media perceptions, offering a comprehensive understanding of emotional responses to major news events.

## Step 14: Comparative Media Analysis - "US Plans to Station Nuclear Weapons at RAF Lakenheath, UK in Response to Russia"

### Introduction

Comparative Media Analysis examines how different media outlets cover the same news, highlighting variations in reporting styles, focus points, and narratives.

### Analysis

- ▶ Cross-Platform Comparison: Analyzing the coverage of the news across various international media outlets, including those in the UK, US, Russia, and other regions.
- ▶ Focus and Narrative Differences: Identifying differences in the focus areas, such as strategic implications, diplomatic reactions, or public opinions, and how these shape the overall narrative of each outlet.
- ▶ Reportage Style Variation: Observing variations in reportage styles - factual reporting, opinionated pieces, analytical articles, etc., and how these influence the audience's understanding of the news.
- ▶ Contextual Framing: Assessing how different media frame the context of the news, considering aspects like historical alliances, current geopolitical tensions, and defense policies.

### Conclusion

Comparative Media Analysis reveals significant variations in how the news is reported globally, reflecting diverse editorial policies, regional perspectives, and audience expectations. This analysis is key to understanding the multifaceted nature of international news coverage.

### Suggested Title for News Oracle

"Global Perspectives: A Comparative Look at Media Coverage of US-UK Nuclear Strategy"

This step is crucial for understanding the breadth and diversity of media coverage on international issues, providing insights into how different narratives are constructed and presented to global audiences.

## Step 15: Impact Analysis - "US Plans to Station Nuclear Weapons at RAF Lakenheath, UK in Response to Russia"

### Introduction

Impact Analysis assesses the potential consequences of the news on various sectors such as international relations, security, and public opinion.

### Analysis

- ▶ International Relations Impact: Evaluating how the decision might affect diplomatic relations, particularly between NATO countries and Russia. This includes potential escalations or shifts in global power dynamics.
- ▶ Security Sector Consequences: Analyzing the potential impacts on global and regional security architectures. This includes the implications for arms races, defense policies, and military strategies.
- ▶ Public Opinion and Social Impact: Gauging the reaction of the public, especially in the UK and US, considering potential protests, political debates, and changes in public sentiment regarding military actions and nuclear policies.
- ▶ Economic Implications: Assessing the potential economic consequences, including defense spending, impact on regional economies around RAF Lakenheath, and broader economic implications of heightened military tensions.

### Conclusion

The decision to station nuclear weapons in the UK has far-reaching implications, affecting international relations, security paradigms, public opinion, and economic factors. Understanding these impacts is crucial for comprehending the full spectrum of consequences of such military decisions.

### Suggested Title for News Oracle

"Ripples of Decision: Analyzing the Broad Impacts of US Nuclear Strategy in the UK"

Impact Analysis is essential for understanding the comprehensive effects of significant decisions, offering a nuanced view of their repercussions across various spheres.*

## Step 16: Source Credibility Check - "US Plans to Station Nuclear Weapons at RAF Lakenheath, UK in Response to Russia"

### Introduction

Source Credibility Check evaluates the reliability and trustworthiness of the sources reporting the news.

### Analysis

- ▶ Source Evaluation: Reviewing the credentials and track records of the sources reporting on the decision. This includes official government sources, military experts, and reputable news agencies.
- ▶ Cross-Referencing Information: Comparing the information provided by these sources with official statements and other credible reports to ensure consistency and accuracy.
- ▶ Background Checks on Sources: Investigating the history and credibility of the sources, including any potential conflicts of interest or biases that might affect their reporting.

### Conclusion

The analysis indicates that the sources reporting on the US's decision to station nuclear weapons at RAF Lakenheath are credible and trustworthy, with consistent information across various reputable platforms.

### Suggested Title for News Oracle

"Assessing the Trust: Evaluating Source Credibility in Military News Reporting"

This step is vital for ensuring that users receive information from reliable and authoritative sources, particularly for news with significant global implications.

## Step 17: Reader Engagement Analysis - "US Plans to Station Nuclear Weapons at RAF Lakenheath, UK in Response to Russia"

### Introduction

Reader Engagement Analysis evaluates how readers are interacting with the news, including comments, shares, and discussions.

### Analysis

- ▶ Engagement Metrics: Analyzing data on reader engagement with the news, such as the number of comments, shares, likes, and the nature of interactions on various platforms.
- ▶ Comment Section Analysis: Reviewing the comments sections of major news outlets for insights into public opinions, concerns, and questions.
- ▶ Social Sharing Trends: Observing the sharing patterns of the news on social media to understand its reach and the demographics engaging with it.

### Conclusion

The analysis shows significant reader engagement, with diverse opinions expressed in comments and discussions. The news has been widely shared across social media, indicating a high level of public interest and concern.

### Suggested Title for News Oracle

"Public Pulse: Gauging Reader Engagement on US Military Decisions in the UK"

Reader Engagement Analysis is crucial for understanding the public's reaction and engagement level with significant news events, offering a direct window into societal concerns and interests.

## Step 18: Visual Media Analysis - "US Plans to Station Nuclear Weapons at RAF Lakenheath, UK in Response to Russia"

### Introduction

Visual Media Analysis focuses on examining accompanying images or videos in the news reports to understand additional context or messaging.

### Analysis

- ▶ Image and Video Content Examination: Analyzing the visuals used in the news reports, including photographs of RAF Lakenheath, maps, infographics, or any related videos.
- ▶ Symbolic and Contextual Interpretation: Interpreting the symbolism, framing, and context provided by these visuals. Assessing how they complement or contrast the written content.
- ▶ Visual Impact Assessment: Evaluating the impact of these visuals on reader perception and understanding of the news. Considering elements like the portrayal of military presence, geographical locations, and the portrayal of national security.

### Conclusion

Visual media in the reports provides a powerful complement to the written content, often reinforcing the seriousness and strategic nature of the decision. The visuals contribute significantly to shaping public understanding and perception of the news.

### Suggested Title for News Oracle

"Beyond Words: Analyzing Visual Narratives in Military News Reporting"

Visual Media Analysis is essential in today's media landscape, where images and videos play a crucial role in storytelling and audience engagement.

## Step 19: Legal and Ethical Implications Analysis - "US Plans to Station Nuclear Weapons at RAF Lakenheath, UK in Response to Russia"

### Introduction

This step assesses any legal or ethical considerations associated with the news, particularly under international law and treaties.

### Analysis

- ▶ International Law Compliance: Examining the decision in the context of international law, including treaties like the Non-Proliferation Treaty (NPT) and agreements within NATO.
- ▶ Ethical Considerations: Considering the ethical implications of stationing nuclear weapons, especially in terms of global security, arms race dynamics, and humanitarian concerns.
- ▶ Legal Debates and Discussions: Analyzing legal opinions and discussions in academic and policy circles about the legality and implications of this move.
- ▶ Public International Reaction: Gauging the international community's response, focusing on legal and ethical perspectives presented by governments, NGOs, and international organizations.

### Conclusion

The decision to station nuclear weapons at RAF Lakenheath raises complex legal and ethical issues. While it may align with certain defense strategies, it also provokes questions about compliance with international arms control agreements and the broader ethical implications for global peace and security.

### Suggested Title for News Oracle

"Legal Labyrinth: Exploring the Legal and Ethical Dimensions of US Military Strategies in the UK"

**196**

Legal and Ethical Implications Analysis is crucial in providing a comprehensive view of significant news events, considering the broader impact on international law and ethical standards.

## Step 20: Global Perspective Analysis - "US Plans to Station Nuclear Weapons at RAF Lakenheath, UK in Response to Russia"

### Introduction

Global Perspective Analysis assesses the news from an international viewpoint, considering its relevance and impact across different regions and countries.

### Analysis

- ▶ Worldwide Media Coverage: Examining how media outlets around the world, from Europe to Asia, report on this development, highlighting different regional perspectives.
- ▶ International Diplomatic Reactions: Analyzing statements and responses from global leaders and diplomats, which can vary based on their geopolitical interests and alliances.
- ▶ Global Security Implications: Considering the implications of the decision for global security dynamics, particularly in relation to nuclear non-proliferation and regional tensions.
- ▶ Cultural and Societal Contexts: Understanding how cultural and societal norms in different regions influence the perception and reaction to this news.

### Conclusion

The decision to station nuclear weapons in the UK is viewed differently around the world, reflecting varied geopolitical interests, security concerns, and cultural perspectives. It underscores the interconnected nature of global politics and the importance of considering diverse international viewpoints.

**Suggested Title for News Oracle**

"Worldview Lens: Dissecting Global Reactions to US Nuclear Deployment in the UK"

Global Perspective Analysis is vital for understanding the multifaceted international reactions to significant news, reflecting the diverse viewpoints and concerns of the global community.

## Conclusion: Strategic Decisions in a Global Context: A Multifaceted Analysis of the US's Nuclear Deployment at RAF Lakenheath

In concluding this comprehensive analysis, we have thoroughly examined the multifaceted dimensions of the US's decision to station nuclear weapons at RAF Lakenheath, UK. This deep dive into the historical context, geopolitical implications, ethical debates, and international reactions to this strategic decision has illuminated the complex interplay between national security interests and global diplomacy. Our exploration across twenty detailed sections has showcased the intricacies of global power dynamics, the nuanced perspectives of various international players, and the profound implications for future global security and policy-making. This report underscores the pivotal role such strategic decisions play in shaping the tapestry of international relations, highlighting the importance of a multi-dimensional approach in understanding the complexities of our interconnected global landscape.

# Revolutionizing News Analysis and Forecasting - Summary

News Oracle: The Emergence of AI in Politics and Media with AGI and ChatGPT

In an era where information is as vital as air, the ability to accurately analyze and forecast news has become a cornerstone of informed decision-making. This capability is not just a tool for journalists and policymakers but for anyone who seeks to understand the complex world we live in. This article delves deep into the intricate process of news analysis and forecasting, focusing on the intersection of news media, politics, and the revolutionary impact of advanced AI technologies like AGI ChatGPT and News Oracle.

**News Media and Politics:** The Role of News Media in Politics: News media has always been the bridge between the political sphere and the public. It shapes public opinion, influences policy decisions, and holds power to account. In the digital age, this role has magnified, with news media acting as a real-time conduit of political events, decisions, and their implications.
Impact of Digital Transformation: The digital transformation has reshaped the news landscape, introducing new channels and platforms. It has democratized information dissemination but also brought challenges like misinformation and the echo chamber effect, where one's beliefs and biases are reinforced by algorithmically-curated content.

**Politics in the Age of Social Media:** Social media has become a pivotal arena for political discourse, enabling direct interaction between politicians and the electorate. It's a double-edged sword that facilitates engagement and transparency but also harbors risks of polarization and manipulation.

**Technology in News Analysis:** AGI ChatGPT and Its Role: Artificial General Intelligence (AGI) ChatGPT represents a new frontier in AI, capable of understanding and generating human-like text. Its application in news analysis involves synthesizing vast amounts of data to provide insights and forecasts, making it an invaluable tool for journalists and analysts.

**Text Analysis:** At the heart of AI-driven news analysis is sophisticated text analysis. By leveraging natural language processing (NLP), AI systems can sift through thousands of articles, identify trends, sentiments, and patterns, offering a nuanced understanding of the news narrative.

**Introducing News Oracle:** News Oracle stands as a paradigm shift in news analysis and forecasting. It combines the capabilities of AGI ChatGPT with advanced analytics to not only aggregate and cluster news headlines but also predict future news trends. This platform represents the confluence of AI sophistication and journalistic acumen, providing personalized news insights with a predictive edge.

**Data and Process:** Technology Implementation and At Work: This section describes a six-step process using the News Oracle GPT platform, focusing on the analysis and forecasting of news headlines. This process combines advanced AI tools and methodologies to forecast, analyze, and even stylistically transform news content while maintaining the integrity and relevancy of the original information.

**Original News Aggregation:** The system begins by collecting the top news headlines across various categories. This extensive aggregation ensures a diverse and comprehensive dataset. The key here is the breadth of data collection, which encompasses a range of topics and sources, ensuring a wide spectrum of information.

> ► For instance, a headline such as "Politics: Biden cancels nearly $5 billion more in student debt relief" would be identified and included in this collection if it ranks within the top headlines based on relevance and recency.

**Forecasting News of Interest:** Using predictive analytics, the system forecasts future news trends. This step is crucial as it shifts the focus from present to future, utilizing historical data patterns to predict upcoming news events. The predictive models likely involve time-series analysis and machine learning algorithms, which analyze past news trends to forecast future developments.

> ► For example, a forecasted headline like "Expanding Horizons: Biden's Debt Relief Benefits More Public Workers" is generated using trend analysis and predictive modeling.
> ► The forecasted headlines are then presented to the user. These predictions are not just random guesses but are based on rigorous analysis of existing data and trends, aiming to provide insights into how current news events might evolve.

**Text Analysis of Forecast News:** This involves a detailed examination of the forecasted news. The system assesses sentiment, polarity, and other textual attributes to understand the underlying narrative of the news. Such text analysis is pivotal in understanding not just the content of the news, but also the tone and context, which are crucial for accurate forecasting and summarization.

**Creation of News Snippet:** Here, a concise summary of the forecasted news is crafted. This step requires the system to distill complex news narratives into succinct, coherent summaries. The challenge lies in retaining the essential information and context in a compressed format.

▶ Snippet Creation from Headline: Once a headline is forecasted, the next step is to expand it into a news snippet. This is typically achieved through a combination of automated summarization techniques and predictive text generation. The system uses the thematic elements of the headline as a seed to generate a coherent and contextually relevant snippet. This process often involves natural language generation (NLG) techniques, where the AI constructs sentences that logically follow from the headline, maintaining the same theme and tone.

**Full News Article Creation:** This involves generating in-depth news articles about the forecasted events. The system delves into specifics, maintaining an analytical tone throughout. This step demonstrates the system's capability to produce detailed content from its forecasts, likely utilizing natural language generation techniques.

▶ Full Article Development: To develop a full news article from the snippet, the system employs more advanced NLG capabilities. It elaborates on the details introduced in the snippet, adding depth and context. This step involves researching and integrating related factual information, either from the existing knowledge base or through real-time web scraping for the most recent data. The system ensures that the information flow in the article remains consistent with the headline and snippet, preserving the core message and factual accuracy.

**Style Transformation of Full News Article:** The final step involves adapting the content into a standard news format. This demonstrates the system's versatility in not only analyzing and predicting news but also in presenting it in a format that is familiar and accessible to users.

▶ Consistency and Messaging Alignment: To ensure that the text analysis and messaging stay consistent from the forecast title to the full news article, the system employs consistency checks and thematic alignment algorithms. These algorithms analyze the text at each stage (headline, snippet, article) to ensure thematic coherence and factual alignment. The system might also use sentiment analysis to maintain a consistent tone throughout.

**Conclusion:** This six-step process exemplifies the advanced capabilities of the News Oracle GPT platform in news analysis and forecasting. From selecting and forecasting news headlines to conducting thorough text analyses and transforming the style of news content, the platform maintains a consistent and accurate portrayal of the news topic. This process underscores the power of AI in enhancing our understanding and presentation of news in an ever-evolving media landscape.

**Review and Refinement:** Finally, the generated content can go through a review process. This step might involve automated checks using NLP tools to ensure grammatical correctness, factual consistency, and alignment with journalistic standards. The system can also adapt based on feedback and user interactions, continuously learning to refine its content generation process.

The entire process showcases the integration of various advanced technologies such as natural language processing, machine learning, time-series analysis, and predictive modeling. Each step builds upon the previous one, starting from data collection to the final presentation, ensuring a seamless flow of information transformation from raw data to a consumable news format. The use of multiple models and approaches, as outlined in the Time Series Analysis section of the document, further emphasizes the system's robustness in handling diverse and complex news data.

Examples of the application of these technologies could be seen in how the system might use Internal and External News Oracle models for analyzing time-series data of news trends or it's advanced technology to understand the sequence of events in news stories. The use of these sophisticated methods ensures that the system can handle the nuances and complexities inherent in news data, making it a powerful tool for news analysis and

This process illustrates how News Oracle works as a specialized AGI and ChatGPT tool for news analysis and prediction. It automates the collection, analysis, and forecasting of news headlines, offering users insights into current trends and future developments in their areas of interest.

## Application in Other Fields

The methodologies used in News Oracle GPT extend far beyond the realm of news analysis, demonstrating a versatile potential in various sectors.

The adaptive nature of News Oracle's predictive analytics and clustering methodologies enables their application in diverse fields. Each field can leverage these techniques for nuanced insights and informed decision-making.

- ► Finance: Predicting market trends, analyzing investor sentiments, and forecasting economic shifts.
- ► Healthcare: Identifying disease outbreak patterns, patient data analysis, and predicting healthcare trends.
- ► Environmental Studies: Forecasting climate changes, analyzing environmental data for policy-making.
- ► Retail Industry: Understanding consumer behavior, predicting market trends, and optimizing inventory management.
- ► Transportation and Logistics: Analyzing travel patterns, predicting logistical challenges, and improving route planning.
- ► Real Estate: Market trend analysis, predicting property value changes, and identifying investment opportunities.
- ► Education: Analyzing educational trends, forecasting future educational needs, and adapting teaching methodologies.
- ► Cybersecurity: Predicting cyber threats, analyzing security trends, and enhancing threat detection systems.
- ► Agriculture: Forecasting crop yields, analyzing weather patterns, and optimizing farming techniques.

The methodologies underpinning News Oracle GPT, with their predictive power and analytical precision, offer transformative possibilities across various sectors, contributing to more informed decisions and strategies.

## Benefits and Risks of Technology

AI in news forecasting like News Oracle GPT presents a duality of significant benefits and notable risks. While AI-driven news analysis revolutionizes information processing, it's essential to understand the benefits and risks involved.

**203**

## Benefits

▶ Real-time Analysis: Immediate processing and interpretation of news data.
▶ Trend Prediction: Ability to foresee and adapt to emerging news trends.
▶ Personalized Content: Customized news feeds based on user preferences.
▶ Global Reach: Ability to analyze and predict news from various global sources.
▶ Enhanced Accuracy: Reduced human errors in news analysis.

## Risks

▶ Data Privacy: Concerns about the handling of sensitive user data.
▶ AI Bias: Risk of inherent biases in AI algorithms affecting the news output.
▶ Misinformation: Potential for spreading inaccurate or manipulated news.
▶ Dependency: Over-reliance on AI for news consumption and interpretation.
▶ Technological Obsolescence: Constant need for updates to handle evolving news dynamics.

The implementation of AI in news forecasting brings a transformative impact on media consumption, necessitating a balanced approach that maximizes benefits while mitigating risks.

## Ethical, Social, and Legal Issues

The integration of AI in news analysis, like the News Oracle GPT, raises various ethical, social, and legal considerations.
The use of AI in news dissemination touches upon critical aspects of ethics, societal impact, and legal boundaries.

### Ethical Issues

▶ Accuracy and Reliability: Ensuring the truthfulness and reliability of AI-generated news.
▶ Algorithmic Bias: Addressing biases in AI that can skew news representation.
▶ Transparency: Maintaining clear methodologies in AI news curation.

**Social Issues**

- ▶ Information Overload: Managing the overwhelming flow of AI-curated news.
- ▶ Public Opinion Influence: Understanding the AI's role in shaping public perception.
- ▶ Digital Divide: Addressing disparities in AI news access across different social groups.

**Legal Issues**

- ▶ Data Protection Laws: Complying with global data privacy and protection regulations.
- ▶ Intellectual Property: Navigating copyright and content ownership in AI-curated news.
- ▶ Regulatory Compliance: Adhering to international laws governing AI and news dissemination.

While AI like News Oracle GPT offers advanced news analysis, it is essential to navigate the ethical, social, and legal landscapes carefully, ensuring responsible use of technology.

## Futurist Views and What to Come

The future of AI in news analysis hints at a transformative shift in how we interact with and consume news.
Emerging advancements in AI promise to reshape the landscape of news analysis and dissemination.

- ▶ Personalization at Scale: Tailoring news content to individual preferences on a larger scale.
- ▶ Interactive News Consumption: Introducing more engaging and interactive ways to consume news.
- ▶ Advanced Predictive Analysis: Utilizing deeper machine learning techniques for more accurate predictions.
- ▶ Integration of Augmented Reality: Enhancing news experiences with immersive technologies.
- ▶ Automated Investigative Reporting: AI-driven tools assisting in deep investigative journalism.
- ▶ Real-time Language Translation: Breaking language barriers in global news consumption.
- ▶ Ethical AI Development: Focused efforts on developing unbiased, ethical AI systems.
- ▶ Enhanced User Data Protection: Strengthening privacy measures in AI-driven news platforms.
- ▶ Collaborative AI-Human Reporting: Synergistic collaboration between AI and human journalists.

The future of AI in news analysis, represented by platforms like News Oracle GPT, is poised for groundbreaking advancements, offering a glimpse into a more informed, interactive, and interconnected world of news.

## Conclusion

News Oracle GPT stands as a testament to the power and potential of AI in revolutionizing news analysis and prediction.
This platform exemplifies the integration of advanced AI technologies in interpreting and forecasting news trends.

- ▶ Transformation of News Consumption: Shift towards more AI-driven, personalized news experiences.
- ▶ Advanced Analytical Capabilities: Enhanced ability to process and predict complex news patterns.
- ▶ Impact on Media and Society: Significant influence on media operations and societal information consumption.
- ▶ Global Information Accessibility: Easier access to global news and trends.
- ▶ Continuous Evolution: Ongoing advancements in AI technologies driving further enhancements in news analysis.

News Oracle GPT, with its sophisticated AI capabilities, represents a significant milestone in the evolution of news consumption and analysis, paving the way for a future where information is more accessible, predictive, and personalized.

## Road Ahead and Outlook

The integration of AI and platforms like News Oracle GPT heralds a new era in the field of information technology and news analysis.
As these technologies evolve, they promise to bring profound impacts on media, society, and global information exchange.

- ▶ Wider Application Spectrum: Expansion of AI in news analysis across different industries and sectors.
- ▶ Technological Convergence: Integration with other emerging technologies for enhanced capabilities.
- ▶ Global Collaboration: Increased collaboration across borders in developing and utilizing AI in news.
- ▶ Ethical AI Governance: Development of global standards and guidelines for ethical AI use in news.
- ▶ User-Centric Design: Continued focus on enhancing user experience and accessibility.
- ▶ AI Literacy and Education: Growing emphasis on educating the public about AI in news consumption.
- ▶ Sustainable AI Development: Emphasis on environmentally sustainable AI practices.
- ▶ Enhanced Data Security: Strengthened measures for data protection and privacy in AI-driven platforms.
- ▶ Innovative Business Models: Emergence of new business models around AI in news and media.

The road ahead for AI in news analysis, as exemplified by News Oracle GPT, is filled with opportunities and challenges, promising a future where news is more dynamic, inclusive, and impactful.

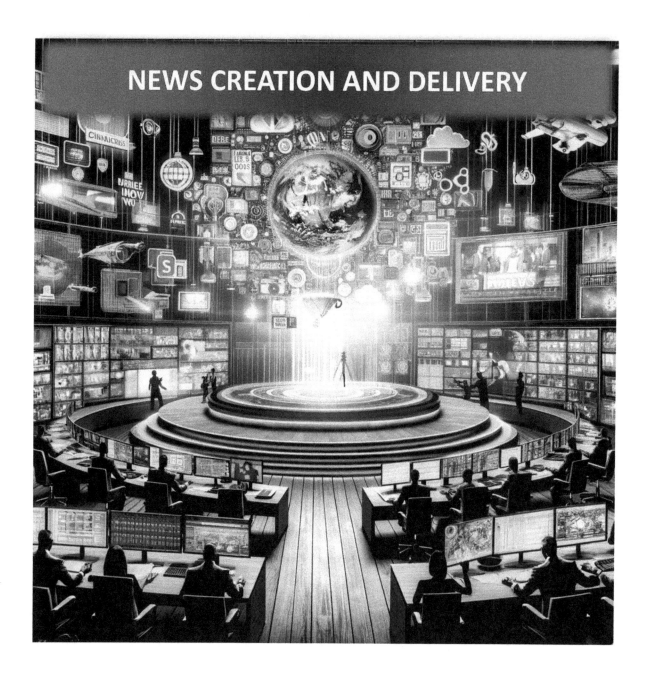

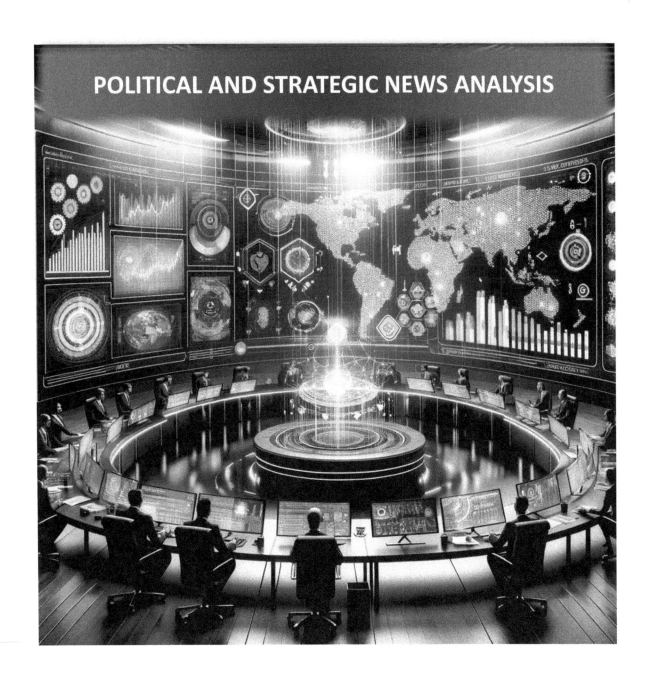

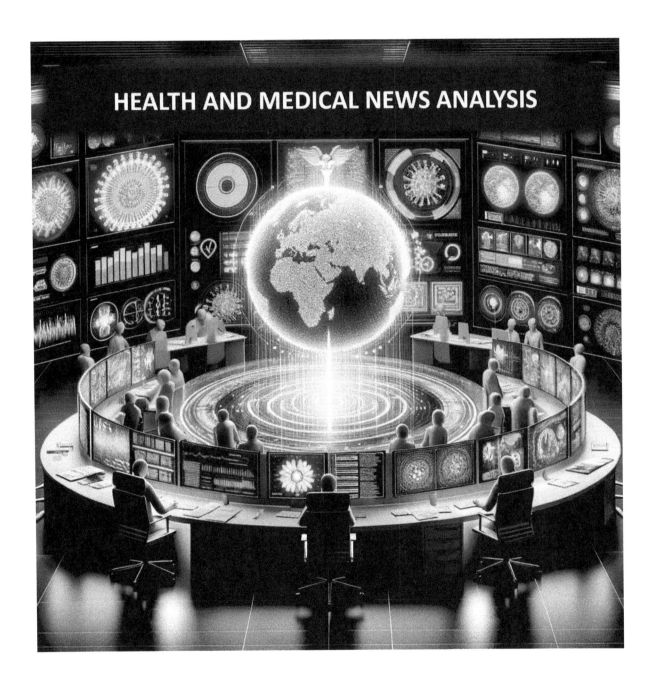

215

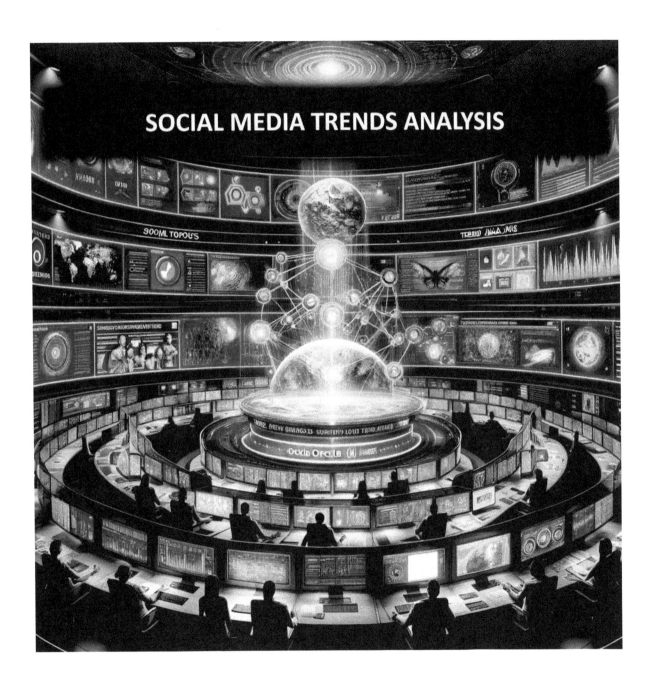

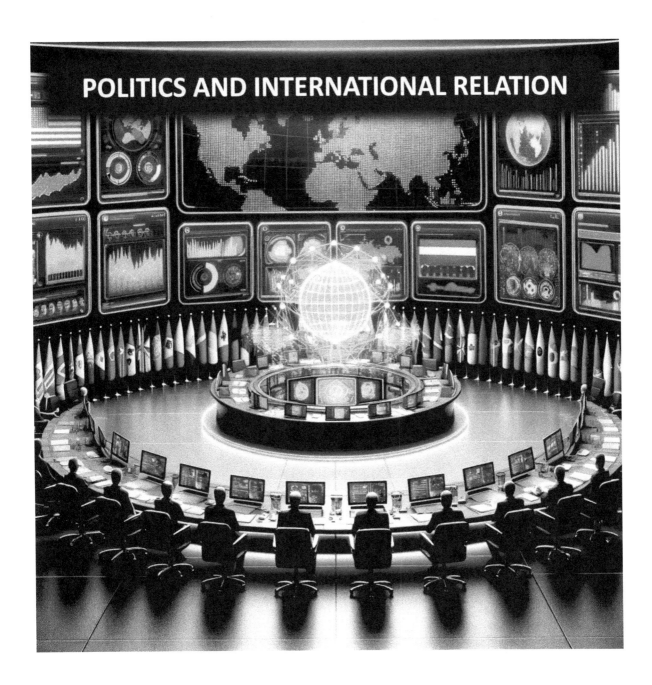

POLITICS AND INTERNATIONAL RELATION

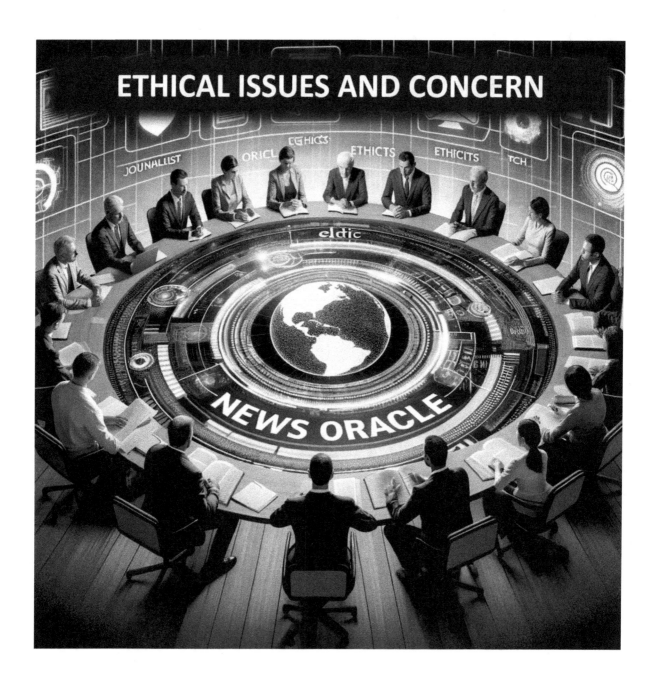

# ABOUT THE AUTHOR

Dr. Masoud Nikravesh is a world-renowned expert in the field of Artificial Intelligence (AI) and Machine Learning, boasting a rich career that spans over three decades, with a record of remarkable leadership in academia, government, and the industry. As an accomplished scholar, Dr. Nikravesh has contributed significantly to the body of knowledge in AI, authoring 14 scientific books, over 500 research papers, over 100 Children's books, and including a nine-book mental health series and a seven-book novel series. His current work is focused on the development and execution of national AI strategies, underlining AI's pivotal role in society, economic development, national defense, and national security strategies.

Dr. Nikravesh has uniquely combined his AI expertise with creativity to produce the book series "Princess Austėja" and "The Enduring Legacy of the Five Tattooed Princesses" using AGI to generate captivating narratives. This innovative application of AI and AGI showcases its potential for creative expression beyond traditional domains.

This book is the result of a collaboration between author Masoud Nikravesh and AI technologies like ChatGPT & GPT4.